NON-WESTERN PERSPECTIVES ON LEARNING AND KNOWING

NON-WESTERN PERSPECTIVES ON LEARNING AND KNOWING

Sharan B. Merriam
and
Associates

KRIEGER PUBLISHING COMPANY
MALABAR, FLORIDA

Original Edition 2007

Printed and Published by
KRIEGER PUBLISHING COMPANY
KRIEGER DRIVE
MALABAR, FLORIDA 32950

> FROM A DECLARATION OF PRINCIPLES JOINTLY ADOPTED BY A COM-
> MITTEE OF THE AMERICAN BAR ASSOCIATION AND A COMMITTEE OF
> PUBLISHERS:
>
> This publication is designed to provide accurate and authoritative information in regard to the subject matter covered. It is sold with the understanding that the publisher is not engaged in rendering legal, accounting, or other professional service. If legal advice or other expert assistance is required, the services of a competent professional person should be sought.

Library of Congress Cataloging-in-Publication Data

Non-Western perspectives on learning and knowing / Sharan B. Merriam and associates.
    p. cm.
    Contents: An introduction to non-Western perspectives on learning and knowing / Sharan B. Merriam — Islam's lifelong learning mandate / Mazalan Kamis and Mazanah Muhammad — American Indian indigenous pedagogy / Paula Gunn Allen — Hinduism and learning / Swathi Nath Thaker — Maori concepts of learning and knowledge / Brian Findsen and Lavinia Tamarua — Buddhist learning: a process to be enlightened / Jienshen Shih — African indigenous knowledge: the case of Botswana / Gabo Ntseane — Liberation theology and learning in Latin America / Simone Conceição and Augusto Marcos Fagundes Oliveira — Adult learning from a Confucian way of thinking / Youngwha Kee — Broadening our understanding of learning and knowing / Sharan B. Merriam.
    ISBN 1-57524-280-X (alk. paper)
     1. Learning—Philosophy. 2. Education—Philosophy. 3. Indigenous peoples—Education. 4. Learning—Cross-cultural studies. I. Merriam, Sharan B.

LB1060.N66 2007
370.15′23—dc22   2006048889

10 9 8 7 6 5

CONTENTS

PREFACE

As with most books, this book has a history behind its inception. A large part of that history has to do with my own growing interest in how other cultures view learning and knowing, an interest fueled by having lived and taught in first Malaysia and then South Korea. While both of these countries are in Asia, they are starkly different in many ways. Malaysia is officially a Moslem country, but with approximately 30% Chinese Malays and 10% Indian Malays it is a very multicultural society wherein Moslem, Hindu, Buddhist, and Christian holidays are celebrated by all. Korea, on the other hand, is a singular population heavily influenced to this day by Confucian philosophy and values. In their journeys to being "modern" societies and in the present period of globalization, both countries have incorporated some Western values and mores and rejected others. Learning for "nation-building" and community benefit in Malaysia competes with learning for personal and career development. In Korea, Confucian values of hierarchy and male dominance are being challenged by more egalitarian relationships (such as between teacher and student) and women's rights.

In addition to living in these two cultures, my interest in this topic has also grown as a result of extensive travel in other parts of the world, as well as being a staff member for the Houle Scholars Program administered by the Adult Education program at the University of Georgia. This Kellogg-funded grant was designed to develop emerging scholars in adult education in the United States, Latin America, and Southern Africa. Our close interaction and annual retreats with young scholars from three parts of the world further widened my own perspective on non-Western orientations to learning and knowing.

These interests culminated in an opportunity to bring scholars together in a symposium at the Adult Education Research Conference (AERC) held in 2005 at the University of Georgia. The title of the symposium was "Challenging the Hegemony of Western Views of Learning" and included five presentations from international scholars representing Hindu, Maori, Islamic, African indigenous knowledge, and Confucian perspectives. It occurred to me while putting the symposium together that the field could really use a book on non-Western perspectives. The symposium was a great success, energizing the entire conference. A number of people who had been at the symposium spoke to me afterward suggesting a book on the topic. One of those people was Mary Roberts, an editor at Krieger Publishing Company. Within a month, I had a proposal into Krieger.

The result is this book wherein I have written the introductory and final chapters. All of the symposium presenters agreed to expand their short conference presentation into full length chapters and three other chapters were commissioned for this book—chapters on Native American, Buddhist, and Latin American perspectives. Decisions as to *which* perspectives to include in this book were a function of making sure we had diverse epistemologies from different parts of the world represented, as well as finding authors indigenous to that perspective to agree to write about it. The focus on *learning and knowing* rather than schooling and formal education challenged us all to think more broadly and philosophically. This non-school orientation, which is particularly relevant to adult educators, does encompass a life-long learning orientation of which schooling is of course a part. Our goal, though, was to explore the larger framework of learning and knowing. Authors were asked to reflect on the following:

1. How is learning thought of and/or what is the purpose of learning from this perspective?

2. What is the nature of knowledge?

   • Is it passed down from one generation to the next? Is it constructed? Both? Is it "spread" across the community?
   • Is there a body of knowledge to be learned? If so, where

is this body of knowledge? In peoples' memories? Embedded in everyday life? In stories and myths? In books? Oral or written or both?

3. How is this knowledge learned? Through practice, memorization, apprenticeship, formal classes?

4. How is it known when one has learned? Who decides that one has learned?

5. What is the role of the teacher? Who can be a teacher?

6. What is the end result of learning? A better, more moral person? A wise person? An independent/interdependent person? A knowledgeable person? A better community? A more equitable society?

7. What is the role of society, community, and/or family in learning?

8. How does this perspective on learning manifest itself in your society today? That is, can we see evidence of this perspective/philosophy in your society today?

The manner in which chapter authors addressed these questions varies from chapter to chapter. Authors were encouraged to embed personal experiences in their chapters and readers will note that there is variation among the chapters on this and other style dimensions—making for varied and interesting reading throughout.

Authors were also asked to assume that readers would know little if anything about their respective tradition. As all of the authors are out of the tradition or intimately familiar with what they were writing about, it was particularly challenging for them to articulate their understandings for others. At the same time, some of the authors, though familiar with and living in the particular tradition, had never thought about these questions in any systematic way. Some turned to literature on the topic and actually "studied" their own tradition in order to write about it for others to read. Finally, for most all of the authors, English is not their first language, a major challenge in conveying philosophical, religious, and even educational terms and concepts.

The first chapter introduces some of the concepts that underlie the book itself such as the Western/non-Western dichotomy and the nature of indigenous knowledge; it argues that broadening our understanding of other ways of knowing and learning is enlightening for us personally as well as in our work as educators. This chapter is followed by the eight chapters on non-Western perspectives. As noted above, an attempt was made to get a broad representation from different parts of the world, rather than being inclusive of every non-Western system that exists in the world. For example, we have a chapter on the Māori of New Zealand but not the Aborigines of Australia; there's a chapter on Native American indigenous pedagogy, but no claim is made to it being inclusive of all Native American, Eskimo, or First Nations (Canada) people; the authors of the chapter on Latin America present from a liberation theology perspective when they and we know there are other perspectives that could have been included. There is no particular order to the chapters other than avoiding grouping primarily religious perspectives or philosophical perspectives or indigenous perspectives together. It is anticipated that readers will want to pick and choose chapters to read in an order that is of most interest to them. The final chapter is my effort to find themes that cut across several perspectives and that are in contrast to a primarily Western orientation to learning and knowing. To that end I discuss the following with reference to the non-Western chapters: (1) Learning is a lifelong journey; (2) What counts as knowledge is broadly defined; and (3) Learning and instruction are holistic and informal.

Finally, I'd like to acknowledge the willingness and hard work of the chapter authors in making this book a reality. All of the original presenters at the AERC symposium in 2005 agreed to "stay on" when their 15-minute presentation turned into a book chapter! Thank you, Mazalan and Mazanah, Brian, Swathi, Gabo, and Youngwha! And thanks to those who joined us to help expand our coverage—Paula, Jienshen, Simone and Augusto, and Lavinia. Thanks also to colleagues in adult edu-

cation who underscored the need for such a book, and to Mary
Roberts at Krieger Publishing who inspired me to get a proposal
together sooner rather than later!

SHARAN B. MERRIAM

Athens, Georgia

CONTRIBUTORS

Paula Gunn Allen—Native American Poet, Novelist and Critic and Professor Emeritus of English/Creative Writing/American Indian Studies, University of California, Los Angeles, United States of America.

Simone C. O. Conceição—Assistant Professor of Adult and Continuing Education, University of Wisconsin-Milwaukee, United States of America.

Brian Findsen—Senior Lecturer and Head of Department of Adult and Continuing Education, University of Glasgow, Scotland.

Mazalan Kamis—Assistant Director, Educational Planning and Policy Research Division, Ministry of Education, Malaysia.

Youngwha Kee—Associate Professor and Head of Department of Lifelong Education, Soongsil University, Seoul, South Korea.

Sharan B. Merriam—Professor of Adult Education, University of Georgia, Athens, Georgia, United States of America.

Mazanah Muhammad—Professor, Department of Professional Development and Continuing Education, Universiti Putra Malaysia, Serdang, Malaysia.

Gabo Ntseane—Senior Lecturer, Department of Adult Education, University of Botswana, Gabarone, Botswana.

Augusto Marcos Fagundes Oliveira—Assistant Professor, State University of Santa Cruz and Center for Higher Education (CESUPI) at Ilheus College, Brazil.

Jienshen F. Shih—Buddhist Monastic and Associate Professor, Department of Education and Human Resource Development, Hsuan Chuang University, Hsin Chu City, Taiwan.

Lavinia Tamarua—Senior Lecturer, School of Education: Te Kura Matauranga, Auckland University of Technology, Ako-ranga Campus, New Zealand.

Swathi Nath Thaker—Ph.D. Student in Adult Education, University of Georgia, Athens, Georgia, United States of America.

CHAPTER 1

An Introduction to Non-Western Perspectives on Learning and Knowing

Sharan B. Merriam

Upon taking my pulse and tapping various "meridian" points along my body, arms, and legs, the elderly Korean gentleman declared my neck and shoulder pain were caused by blocked energy flow in one of my energy "channels." He then affixed a small round patch at a precise point on the third finger of my left hand. Within a couple of hours my pain had greatly subsided. So went my encounter with Eastern medicine, a perspective based on invisible channels of energy that must be kept open and in balance. Many Westerners would of course dismiss this practice as nonscientific and find nonmedical explanations for my apparent improvement. To restrict one's understanding of the world to Western science precludes learning and perhaps benefiting from what other perspectives have to offer.

So too with learning and knowing. We know very little about other epistemological systems as we are immersed in our own Western orientation to learning and knowing. Beginning with behaviorist research in the early decades of the 20th century, most of what we know about learning and adult learning has been shaped by what counts as knowledge in a Western paradigm. Embedded in this perspective are the cultural values of privileging the *individual* learner over the collective, and promoting *autonomy* and *independence* of thought and action over community and interdependence. In adult learning theory, andragogy, self-directed learning, and much of the literature on transformational learning position self-direction, independence, rational discourse, and reflective thought as pinnacles of adult learning.

However, we need only look more closely within our borders to Native Americans and beyond the borders of North America and Western Europe to find major systems of thought and beliefs embedded in entirely different cultural values and epistemological systems, some of which pre-date Western perspectives by thousands of years and encompass most of the world's peoples. This book is a sampling of these other perspectives and includes chapters on Islamic, Native American, Buddhist, Māori, Hindu, African indigenous knowledge, Latin American, and Confucian perspectives.

As a context for considering these perspectives, this introductory chapter explores some of the key concepts important to understanding non-Western perspectives. I first discuss the Western/non-Western dichotomy itself, admittedly an imprecise way to categorize these perspectives. Next I explore the concepts of culture and indigenous knowledge. The final section of this introductory chapter makes a case for the importance of considering non-Western perspectives on learning and knowing.

THE WESTERN/NON-WESTERN DICHOTOMY

Most of what we know about learning has been studied and written about by scholars in "Western" countries, that is scholars primarily from North America, Western Europe, Australia, and New Zealand. This book, however, centers perspectives that are embedded in contexts decidedly non-Western. There are problems, of course, with classifying epistemological systems according to Western or non-Western. The dichotomy itself is a particularly Western concept. Dichotomies such as "mind-body," "nature-nurture," "emotion-reason," and "human-animal" are in fact an "obsession . . . that runs through Western intellectual history" (Nisbett, 2003, p. 154). Further, the many indigenous peoples who live in "Western" countries such as Native Americans in North America or the Aboriginals of Australia do not adhere to a Western perspective. Also problematic is the suggestion that "Western" is the gold standard against which we measure non-Western thus depriving non-Westerners of having legitimate knowledge apart from Western norms. So why use this dichotomy? We use the terms because it is a shorthand means of referring to the unfamiliar and because we can most readily understand these unfamiliar perspectives by contrasting them with what we *do* know, that is, the Western tradition. Further, as Reagan (2005, p. 11) notes, "the biases inherent in the terms are in fact a significant and telling component of the phenomenon that we are concerned with studying. . . . Thus, what begins as a false dichotomy can emerge as an effective way of challenging and reforming racist and ethnocentric assumptions and biases."

Scholars have traced the construction of Western thought back to Greece. Plato, for example, advocated the separation of thought and emotions, "decreeing that to study a phenomenon, one must remove oneself, at least emotionally, from it. To remove oneself emotionally from something or somebody is to view that thing or person instrumentally—as something that one can use and/or exploit" (Ntuli, 2002, p. 56). Classical Greek culture further promoted "personal freedom, individuality, and objective thought" (Nisbett, 2003, p. 30), values brought to Europe and extended throughout the world through European colonization. The 17th-century French philosopher Descartes declared that "I [that is, my mind, by which I am what I am] is entirely and truly distinct from my body" and that "body, figure, extension, motion, and place are merely fictions of my mind" (Descartes, 1960 [1637], pp. 165, 118, cited in Michelson, 1998, p. 218). This separation of the mind and body was reinforced by 18th-century Enlightenment philosophers who believed that knowledge could be obtained through reason alone; other sources of knowledge at that time such as faith, tradition, and authority were rejected by many.

Independence, separation, and hierarchies characterize a Western perspective, a view in direct contrast to most non-Western worldviews. African thought, for example, "sees life as a cycle; the world as an interconnected reality; human beings, plants, animals and the universe as one interconnected whole, and that our survival depends on how these forces interact with each other." Further,

> The beginning and meaning of life lie within the world of myth, and these myths are given form through rituals. For these rituals to be effective, dances and other cultic acts are performed, and art objects are created to give form and potency to the ritual. In other words, songs are composed, dances performed, and sculptures and other art objects are created to support rituals.
>
> These rituals accompany us throughout our lives, from birth, through initiation ceremonies, weddings, festivals, funerals and many other events. The purpose of the events is, in the case of African people, to secure the place of humans in the wider scheme of things. The African believes that the world we live in is sacred in nature and that our role is to preserve and protect everything in it. (Ntuli, 2002, p. 58)

The domination of Western thought is sustained through "scientific" research; colonization of the world is now intellectual and conceptual. Indeed, the "power of Western science involves its ability to depict its findings as universal knowledge. Modernist science produces universal histories, defines civilization, and determines reality: such capabilities legitimate particular ways of seeing and, concurrently, delegitimate others" (Semali & Kincheloe, 1999, p. 31). Thus a key to understanding this Western/non-Western dichotomy is the concept of knowledge—what counts as legitimate knowledge, who constructs this knowledge about whom, and how is this knowledge transmitted? For colonized peoples, the knowledge that counts has been the knowledge of their European or American colonizers. Native American education in America today, for example, is about acquiring a set of technical skills such that the learners can contribute to the social and economic structures of society. According to Deloria's (2001) analysis, the current educational system separates knowledge into two parts—professional expertise and personal growth. This is problematic for Indian students "because in traditional Indian society there is no separation; there is, in fact, a reversal of the sequencer in which non-Indian education occurs; in traditional society the goal is to

ensure personal growth and then to develop professional expertise" (p. 43). It is not only First Nations peoples who see "learning as a personal journey towards wholeness" (Hart, 1996,
p. 64). Hindu, Confucian, and Islamic traditions also focus on
wholistic development though toward somewhat different ends;
further, this is a *lifelong* journey from birth to death (see chapters in this volume).

The tyranny of Western science precludes its ability to hear,
see, or feel other possibilities or to readily accommodate change
within its systems. Since changes are the result of long periods
of research and testing, Western science lacks the flexibility of
other systems of knowing and learning. Many other traditions
have traditionally passed on knowledge orally rather than in
written form; sometimes "no firm conclusions are reached. . . .
The storyteller simply states that what he or she has said was
passed down by elders or that he or she marveled at the phenomenon and was unable to explain it further. It is permissible
within the Indian context to admit that something mysterious
remains after all is said and done. Western science seems incapable of admitting that anything mysterious can exist or that
any kind of behavior or experience can remain outside its ability
to explain" (Deloria, 2001, p. 124).

But there are even more sinister consequences of privileging
Western knowledge and science over other systems. Hoppers
(2002), for example, writes that "the exclusivity that accompanied the rational and linear frameworks of Western knowledge
has, in practice, meant that cosmologies that did not fit into that
framework were dismissed and ridiculed" (p. 13). She goes on
to point out that "the knowledge of 'Other' peoples, of women,
and of all phenomena that could not be measured by the different scientific methods, were all undermined or destroyed" (p.
13) first by colonialism and later with modernization.

The separation of knowledge from its context and its codification according to Western science has had an impact on
educational thought and practice. Education has become syn-
onymous with "schooling," such that adult learners have a
difficult time thinking of their learning as anything but participation in formal classes. Informal learning which adults engage

in on a daily basis is rarely identified as important learning. "Western epistemological tyranny and the oppressive educational practices that follow it" (Semali & Kincheloe, 1999, p. 31) has resulted in our overlooking rich sources of knowledge. For example,

> Western epistemological exports to Africa . . . tend to limit reality to appearances with which they [Westerners] seek to justify, mostly without explanation, the so-called absolute and irrefutable truth. For Africans, the search for truth goes beyond appearances into some deep understanding of why the truth is truth. Sometimes the search for truth may be mystified as [when] recourse may be made to traditional religious performances. Among the Yoruba in Nigeria, the *ifa* oracle of divination may be used to determine what the truth is. Magical understanding and interpretation of the truth is accepted in Africa and this is connected to the way in which people know. (Fasokun, Katahoire, Oduaran, 2005, pp. 63–64)

Further, if we only apply our Western understandings of learning, we cannot understand what learning means for those in non-Western cultures. For example, in a study of self-directed learning in the Korean context, a context greatly influenced by Confucianism, most of the Western values were rejected (Nah, 2000). Rather, "a person becoming independent of his or her parents, teachers or other people, tends to be considered threatening [to] the stability of a community he or she belongs to. . . . Becoming independent without being interdependent passes for immaturity or self-centeredness" (p. 18). Moreover, as a country that has faced numerous enemies, "collectivism and collaboration are taught from one's childhood as one of the most important survival skills and moral virtues" (p. 18).

In yet another example, the notion of transformational learning from a Buddhist thought system involves "increased insight into the nature of reality result[ing] in an understanding of the interconnection of all living beings and a decrease in human suffering" (Brooks, 2000, p. 166). Brooks goes on to point out that "although Buddhism is a part of mainstream institutional culture in many Asian nations, it stands as an alternative to the mainstream in the West" (p. 166).

In summary, the Western/non-Western dichotomy, while not perfect, does capture what this book attempts to do—bring to the fore new ways of thinking about learning and how these perspectives differ from what we have grown up believing about learning, knowing, education, the teacher-student relationship, and so on. The presentation of non-Western perspectives challenges the hegemony of Western ways of knowing. We now turn to two other important concepts in positioning the chapters in this book.

CULTURE AND INDIGENOUS KNOWLEDGE

There are hundreds of definitions of culture. Basically, culture consists of the shared behavior and symbolic meaning systems of a group of people. It is, as Hofstede (cited in Samovar & Porter, 1991, p. 51) writes, "the collective programming of the mind which distinguishes the members of one category of people from another." Banks and Banks (1997, p. 8) have defined it as follows:

> The essence of a culture is not its artifacts, tools, or other tangible cultural elements but how the members of the group interpret, use, and perceive them. It is the values, symbols, interpretations, and perspectives that distinguish one people from another in modernized societies; it is not material objects and other tangible aspects of human societies.

Interwoven with culture is language. Language is "culture expressing itself in sound" (Williams, cited in Brock-Utne, 2002, p. 245) and it is the source of our identity growing up, an identity that will always define us as a member of a sociocultural family. In an interesting comparison of Western and Eastern thought systems, Nisbett (2003) finds language mirrors the differences: "Western languages encourage the use of nouns, which results in categorization of objects, and Eastern languages encourage the use of verbs, with the consequence that it is relationships that are emphasized" (p. 155). Further, Western thought is more analytic which leads to verbalizing objects, their attributes and categorization; Eastern thought is more holistic and relational which helps explain "a long tradition in the East of equating silence rather than speech with knowledge" (p. 211).

Unfortunately, Western colonizing also brought with it an educational system requiring the learning of languages of the colonizer. For decades Native Americans, Aboriginal and Māori peoples, many people in Latin America and in British colonies such as India were forced to learn in the language of their colonizers, suppressing their own cultural identity as expressed in their native languages. As language is an expression of culture and of systems of thought, non-Western traditions of learning were devalued, marginalized, and often brutally suppressed. While efforts have been underway for some time now in reclaiming and valuing native languages, and indeed, employing these languages in schooling, part of the power of Western domination continues to be linguistic. Witness how English is the preferred language of the Internet, of multinational companies, and so on. This book itself is a good example of language being a cultural and epistemological issue. The eight chapters on non-Western perspectives are all in English and a number of authors had difficulty conveying the true sense of certain indigenous concepts into English.

While we often link "Western" and "culture" together, "there is no single 'Western' culture in any really meaningful sense; rather, there are many different and distinct cultures that share certain elements of a common historical background that are manifested in different ways in the present" (Reagan, 2005, p. 37). What linking "Western" and "non-Western" to culture does is to provide a kind of shorthand for comparing two epistemological systems. For example, Wildcat (2001) compares Aristotelian or Western with Indigenous or American Indian politics and ethics. From a Western perspective, the definition of "persons" is limited to human beings; a Native American perspective finds this definition far too limiting and includes other living beings and natural objects into the community of persons.

In a Western view, society is equated with the political state, but from an indigenous perspective society encompasses the entire ecosystem.

Jegede (1999) lays out a similar comparison of African and Western systems of thought. In African culture "orality predominates," whereas in Western thought knowledge is "documented." As another example, in Africa, "learning is communal," but in the West, "learning is an individual enterprise" (p. 125). Finally, drawing from an Asian cultural perspective, Abdullah (1996), a management consultant in Malaysia, compares what she calls "individualistic" or "more Western" with "collectivistic" or "more Eastern" cultural interpretations of values. With regard to group versus individual preference, for example, Westerners value freedom and independence whereas Easterners value belonging, harmony, family, security, and guidance; success in the West is materialistic but in the East it is relationship/friendship based; communication style in a more Western cultural orientation is direct, to the point, and emphasizes clarity, whereas in a more Eastern culture communication is subtle, indirect, and often employs a third party. Understanding these and other differences in values, Abdullah points out, is crucial to managing a multinational and multicultural workplace.

What is presented as "Western," "Native American," "African," "Latin American," or "Eastern" values and systems of thought capture, imperfectly of course, some of the differences that in turn affect not only how we see the world, but how learning experiences are interpreted. For example, in a study of the role of cultural values in shaping older adult learning in Malaysia, participants spoke of learning as a spiritual or philosophical quest, and as "a responsibility and a means of giving back to their communities" (Merriam & Muhammad, 2000, p. 60). As another example, Wang (2006a) found that Chinese students' experiences in online courses in U.S. universities were shaped by the Chinese cultural values of resorting to silence or passive learning, being hardworking and diligent, preferring formal or content-oriented discussion, exhibiting deference to the teacher and concern for others, and worrying about "losing face."

   An integral part of culture and another concept important
for understanding learning and knowing from non-Western perspectives is that of *indigenous knowledge*. Like culture, indigenous knowledge has been defined in numerous ways, and has
been critiqued for conveying "deeply ingrained idealizations as
well as negative prejudices" (Antweiler, 2004, p. 5). Most definitions of indigenous knowledge include "local or community
knowledge that is commonly generated and transmitted over a
period of time in geographic and historic space" (Fasokun,
Katahoire, & Oduaran, 2005, p. 61). It is knowledge generated
to deal with local problems and issues "related to health, farming, warfare, education, culture and the environment" (p. 61).
Indigenous knowledge "is not just about woven baskets, handi-
craft for tourists or traditional dances *per se*. Rather, it is about
excavating the technologies behind those practices and artifacts" (Hoppers, 2002, p. 9). This is knowledge produced by
people who, according to the World Council of Indigenous
Peoples, "occupied lands prior to populations who now share
or claim such territories"; indigenous peoples may also "possess
a distinct language and culture" (Semali & Kincheloe, 1999,
p. 40). Dei, Hall, and Rosenberg (2000) point out that many
indigenous cultures value the following: "seeing the individual
as part of nature; respecting and reviving the wisdom of elders;
giving consideration to the living, the dead, and future generations; sharing responsibility, wealth, and resources within the
community; and embracing spiritual values, traditions and practices reflecting connections to a higher order, to the culture, and
to the earth" (p. 6).
   Because indigenous knowledge is often contrasted with
Western (scientific) knowledge, some writers prefer the term "local knowledge." The comparison with Western knowledge "implies many dichotomies (e.g. us/them, west/rest, rationality/
magic, universal/particular, tradition/modernity)" (Antweiler,
2004, p. 3). Another problem with the term "indigenous," Antweiler (2004) points out, is that "many environmentalists and
some social movements portray indigenous peoples as 'eco-
saints'. Some see their knowledge as an antidote to some of the
world's problems. . . . These idealizations are as distorting as

earlier views of the 'primitive mind' or 'traditional mentality' seen as irrational and thus as a scapegoat for underdevelopment" (p. 6). Nevertheless, the term "indigenous knowledge" is the more commonly used term among other possibilities.

Indigenous knowledge differs from official, academic knowledge in several ways. First, it is organic in the sense that it is generated within the daily lives of people in local context rather than "by planned procedures and rules" (George, 1999, p. 80). This knowledge is typically passed on from one generation to the next in oral, rather than written form. So too, the "pedagogy" of indigenous knowledge differs from traditional schooling or education. Knowledge is conveyed through "story-telling, poetry, metaphor, myth, ceremony, dreams and art; and honoring indigenous elders as 'cultural professor'" (Graveline, 2005, p. 308). Underscoring the nature of indigenous knowledge, Brock-Utne (2002, p. 239) recounts the African proverb, "When an elder dies in Africa, it is a library that burns." Brock-Utne explains:

> The truth is even more tragic, however. For in the event of a library burning, other copies of the books lost may be found, and another library set up. Given Africa's situation of poor geographical, historical and linguistic intercommunication, and with oral traditions being the dominant mode of transmission to this day, it can be said that an elder's death is the equivalent of the burning of a unique and living manuscript. Day by day, such living manuscripts pass away, and Africa's school system thus loses more of the roots of its cultural truth. (p. 239)

As many writers have pointed out, we have much to learn from indigenous knowledge systems throughout the world. What has until recently prevented us from accessing and learning from these systems is

> "Western" knowledge production—it is self-contained, self-sustaining, handy, convenient, and even tinged with a sense of righteousness. . . . Hermetically sealed, the closed system of "Western" knowledge production has been institutionalized, in a matter of several hundred years, to such a degree as to dis-

miss indigenous knowledges based on thousands of years of experience, analysis, and reflection as primitive (Allen, 1989; Deloria, 1997; Harjo & Bird, 1997). It is . . . intellectual apartheid.
(Rains, 1999, p. 317)

In summary, non-Western perspectives on learning and
knowing include, for example, indigenous knowledge systems
such as found in Africa, in Latin America, in Native American
and First Nations peoples of North America, and in Māori
people of New Zealand and Aboriginal people of Australia.
Typically however, major philosophical or religious systems of
thought such as Buddhism, Islam, Hinduism, Confucianism,
and so on are labeled "non-Western" rather than indigenous. Of
course how we group or label these systems is not what is important. What is important is that by becoming acquainted with
other ways of learning and knowing we enrich our understanding of learning, and ultimately our practice with adults.

EXPANDING OUR UNDERSTANDING OF
LEARNING AND KNOWING

Graduate schools of education that prepare teachers, instructors, and facilitators to teach learners from preschool
through post-secondary institutions through to older adults in
retirement all operate from a worldview that privileges Western
knowledge codified in Western textbooks, academic journals,
and conference proceedings. The hegemony of the Western "scientific" perspective is also in evidence in the schools and universities of the non-Western world where Western textbooks, theories, and research are valued over local or regional resources.
One's own perspective is put aside, at least temporarily, while
one struggles to absorb (often memorize) the officially sanc-
tioned knowledge.

Certainly a more palatable approach would be to uncover
and acknowledge what people already know, then see how exposure to another system can enhance their development and
their practice. Baumgartner, Karanth, Aurora, and Ramaswamy

(2004) in a chapter titled, "In Dialogue with Indigenous Knowledge: Sharing Research to Promote Empowerment of Rural Communities in India," discuss their success with merging the indigenous knowledge system with "external sources of knowledge" (p. 222). The indigenous knowledge, or "tacit knowledge is experience-bound, either individually internalized or collectively shared. Explicit knowledge is exchanged through dialogue, making it accessible for systematized and shared understanding. A society can promote effective learning by paying attention to the links between spheres of tacit and explicit knowledge" (p. 222).

Not understanding another's perspective can lead to marginalizing if not oppressing the "other." In a study of professional development of Native American women for example, Mott (2004, p. 133) writes, "One woman relayed her story of being chastised by her supervisor for her "lack of competition" on the job. She quietly shared that she tried to explain her behavior as part of her Cherokee ethos of group support and collaboration instead of individual competition 'when he told me I should forget I'm Indian and remember I have a job to do.'"

Being open to how someone with a worldview different from one's own learns and instructs can be rewarding. Cahill (Cahill & Collard, 2003) recounts how she came to realize that Aboriginal people of Western Australia learn by watching and listening rather than asking questions. A non-Aboriginal teacher asked some Aboriginal friends to teach her a card game she had seen them play:

> The friends readily agreed, sat Glenda down at the card table, and proceeded to play the game as before—but none of the expected commentary was forthcoming. . . . She was expected to watch carefully and to work the game out for herself. As Glenda later related the incident, she reflected that this approach to learning can take a bit longer, but that it results in deeper and fuller understanding—she picked up tactics about the game and traps to avoid and ended up learning much more than just rules and procedures (from Cahill, 1999, p. 20). (Cahill & Collard, 2003, p. 213).

Even in this increasingly diverse and multicultural world, educators might argue that since the Western tradition has been codified, legitimized, and exported throughout the world as *the* perspective from which to operate, why bother to consider yet other systems of learning? The purpose of examining other systems is not to replace the Western tradition, but to expand our understanding of learning and knowing so that our practice as educators can be more inclusive and effective. This is in fact the goal of a recent special issue of the journal, *Advances in Developing Human Resources* (2006). The entire issue is devoted to presenting different worldviews of adult learning in the workplace including Hindu, Buddhist, Confucian, Islamic, Jewish, Russian Orthodoxy, Mormon, Ojibwe, Māori, and Ubantu. As the editors comment:

> Most human resource development (HRD) professionals and students in the United States and other industrialized nations are schooled in traditional Western philosophies of education but are now dealing with others who look at the world through different perspectives. This issue of *Advances* presents a range of philosophies and/or views and/or approaches to adult learning with a focus on implications for HRD in the workplace. It provides a summary of some worldviews to help readers understand and appreciate other educational models, perspectives, approaches, and philosophies. (Johansen & McLean, 2006, p. 321)

Such exposure can impact our practice as adult educators in a number of ways. First, we might rethink our purposes as educators from largely transmitters of "validated Western information" to "a more compelling form of analysis . . . engaging students in the interpretation of various knowledges and modes of knowledge production" (Semali & Kincheloe, 1999, p. 34). Closely aligned with this purpose is that considering other ways of knowing leads us to examine how knowledge is produced, whose interests are being served by this knowledge, and how knowledge comes to be validated or "official." "Such an awareness is too often absent in Western education. In mainstream pedagogies we are taught to believe that the knowledge we consider official and valid has been produced in a neutral, noble, and altruistic manner. Such a view dismisses the cultural and power-related dimensions of knowledge production" (Semali & Kincheloe, 1999, p. 34).

Yet another purpose in becoming familiar with other knowledge systems is the benefit this knowledge will have in affecting our practice with learners having other than Western worldviews. Antone and Gamlin (2004), for example, argue that to be effective, literacy programs with Aboriginal people (a term they use to refer to First Nations, Inuit, and Métis persons and collectivities) must be more than "reading, numeracy and writing which is typically directed towards gaining access to mainstream employment" (p. 26). Rather, Aboriginal literacy

> is about sustaining a particular worldview and about the survival of a distinct and vital culture. Being literate is about resymboliz-ing and reinterpreting past experience, while at the same time honouring traditional values. Being literate is about *living* these values in contemporary times. Being literate is about *visioning* a future in which an Aboriginal *way of being* will continue to thrive. Meaningful Aboriginal literacy will develop and find ex-pression in everything that is done. Consequently Aboriginal lit-eracy programs must reflect a broad approach that recognizes the unique ways that Aboriginal people represent their experience and knowledge. (p. 26, emphasis in original)

Another example of how having some familiarity with other worldviews can impact our practice as adult educators is in understanding how many Asian students view aspects of the teaching/learning transaction. Their reticence to question or speak out in our classes is due to years of training that speaking out might cause someone (the teacher in particular) to lose face; the accepted strategy is to personally approach the teacher out-side class. Further, silence for Asians is a positive trait as Con-fucius wrote that " 'He who knows does not speak, he who speaks does not know' " (Nisbett, 2003, p. 211). As Liu (2001, p. 190) points out, "silence is used by east Asian collectivists as an indication of strength, power and disagreement, whereas in-dividualists see it as an indication of weakness, shyness, or trouble." Finally, Wang (2006b) notes that for a Chinese student, sharing something personal in our adult education classes is seen as a sign of weakness, a loss of manners, or an attempt to seek help.

A final value in expanding our understanding of learning to include perspectives outside of our traditional Western views is that we will be personally enriched. Not only does such exposure lead to reflecting on our own ideas in new ways, but hearing others' stories about their learning contributes to our own meaning-making. While we can

> acknowledge that no story perfectly evokes all that is true about our lives, . . . we must also acknowledge that the more stories we have available to us, the richer are our resources. . . . the more voices and narratives to which we listen, the more abundantly we experience our lives. In fact, we often find that as different from ourselves as we may imagine the others who create those narratives to be, we can still find that the stories from their lives reflect something true about our own. In that case, for both their differences and their similarities, we can hardly afford to let some voices remain marginal and silenced and other voices dominate. (Brooks, 2000, p. 169)

So for a variety of reasons, exposure to non-Western modes of learning and knowing will not only enlarge our own individual understanding, but enhance our practice as educators.

SUMMARY

"The problem with the concept of world-view is that too often we accept that it means we all stand on the same world and view *it* differently, when, in fact, what we should learn from this phrase is that there may, indeed, be fundamentally different worlds to view" (West, 1996, p. 2). These words capture what this chapter, this book, is intended to do—describe the different worlds that non-Westerners have constructed with regard to learning and knowing. In this chapter I first dealt with the admittedly problematic dichotomy of Western/non-Western explaining that it is merely a shorthand way of presenting differing views (or different worlds as the above quote suggests). The second section of the chapter included a discussion of culture and indigenous knowledge, concepts important to contextualizing the views presented in subsequent chapters. Finally, I suggested that there are a number of reasons why we as educators should attend to other than Western systems of learning and knowing, and how knowledge of these systems might enlarge our understanding of learning and enhance our practice.

REFERENCES

Abdullah, A. (1996). *Going glocal: Cultural dimensions in Malaysian management*. Kuala Lumpur, MY: Malaysian Institute of Management.

Antone, E. M., & Gamlin, P. (2004). Foundations for Aboriginal adult literacy. In D. E. Clover (Ed.), *Proceedings of the Joint International Conference of the 45th Adult Education Research Conference and the Canadian Association for the Study of Adult Education* (pp. 25–30). Victoria, CA: University of Victoria.

Antweiler, C. (2004). Local knowledge theory and methods: An urban model from Indonesia. In A. Bicker, P. Sillitoe, & J. Pottier (Eds.), *Investigating local knowledge: New directions, new approaches* (pp. 1–34). Hants, England and Burlington, Vermont: Ashgate Publishing Limited.

Banks, J. A., & Banks, C. A. M. (1997). *Multicultural education: Issues and perspectives* (3rd ed.). Boston, MA: Allyn & Bacon.

Baumgartner, R., Karanth, G. K., Aurora, G. S., & Ramaswamy, V. (2004). In dialogue with indigenous knowledge: Sharing research to promote empowerment of rural communities in India. In A. Bicker, P. Sillitoe, & J. Pottier (Eds.), *Investigating local knowledge: New directions, new approaches* (pp. 207–232). Hants, England and Burlington, Vermont: Ashgate Publishing Limited.

Brock-Utne, B. (2002). Stories of the Hunt—Who is writing them? In C. A. O. Hoppers, (Ed.), *Indigenous knowledge and the integration of knowledge systems* (pp. 237–254). Claremont, South Africa: New Africa Books.

Brooks, A. K. (2000). Cultures of transformation. In A. L. Wilson &

E. R. Hayes (Eds.), *Handbook of adult and continuing education* (pp. 161–170). San Francisco: Jossey-Bass.

Cahill, R., & Collard, G. (2003). *Deadly ways to learn . . . a yarn about some learning we did together. Comparative Education, 39*(2), 211–219.

Dei, G. J., Hall, B. L., & Rosenberg, D. G. (2000). Introduction. In G. J. Dei, B. L. Hall, & D. G. Rosenberg (Eds.), *Indigenous knowledges in global contexts* (pp.3–17). Toronto: University of Toronto Press

Deloria, V. Jr. (2001). Knowing and understanding. In V. Deloria, Jr. & D. R. Wildcat, (Eds.), *Power and place: Indian education in America* (pp. 41–46). Golden, Colorado: American Indian Graduate Center and Fulcrum Resources

Fasokun, T., Katahoire, A., & Oduaran, A. (2005). *The psychology of adult learning in Africa.* Hamburg, Germany: UNESCO Institute for Education and Pearson Education South Africa.

George, J. M. (1999). Indigenous knowledge as a component of the school curriculum. In L. M. Semali & J. L. Kincheloe (Eds.), *What is indigenous knowledge? Voices from the academy* (pp. 79–94), New York: Falmer Press.

Graveline, F. J. (2005). Indigenous learning. In L. M. English (Ed.), *International encyclopedia of adult education* (pp. 304–309). New York: Palgrave Macmillan.

Hart, M. A. (1996). Sharing circles: Utilizing traditional practice methods for teaching, helping, and supporting. In S. O'Meara & D. A. West (Eds). *From our eyes: Learning from indigenous peoples* (pp. 59–72). Toronto: Garamond Press.

Hoppers, C. A. O. (2002). Indigenous knowledge and the integration of knowledge systems. In C. A. O. Hoppers (Ed.), *Indigenous knowledge and the integration of knowledge systems* (pp. 2–22), Claremont, South Africa: New Africa Books.

Jegede, O. J. (1999). Science education in nonwestern cultures: Towards a theory of collateral learning. In L. M. Semali & J. L. Kincheloe (Eds.), *What is indigenous knowledge? Voices from the academy* (pp. 119–142). New York: Falmer Press.

Johansen, B-C. P., & McLean, G. W. (2006). Worldviews of adult learning in the workplace: A core concept in human resource development. *Advances in Developing Human Resources, 8*(3), 321–328.

Liu, J. (2001). *Asian students' classroom communication patterns in U.S. universities: An emic perspective.* Westport, CT: Ablex.

Merriam, S. B., & Muhammad, M. (2000). How cultural values shape learning in older adulthood: The case of Malaysia. *Adult Education Quarterly, 51*(1), 45–63.

Michelson, E. (1998). Re-membering: The return of the body to experiential learning. *Studies in Continuing Education, 20*(2), 217–233.

Mott, V. W. (2004). The role of culture in continuing professional education: An examination of epistemology and reflection among Native American women. In R. M. Cervero, B. Courtenay, T. Hixson, & J. Valente (Eds.), *Global perspectives in adult education, Volume IV* (pp. 127–137). University of Georgia press, Athens, GA.

Nah, Y. (2000). Can a self-directed learner be independent, autonomous and interdependent?: Implications for practice. *Adult Learning, 18*, 18–19, 25.

Nisbett, R. E. (2003). *The geography of thought: How Asians and Westerners think Differently . . . and why.* New York: The Free Press.

Ntuli, P. P. (2002). Indigenous knowledge systems and the African renaissance. In C. A. O. Hoppers (Ed.), *Indigenous knowledge and the integration of knowledge systems* (pp. 53–66). Claremont, South Africa: New Africa Books.

Rains, F. V. (1999). Indigenous knowledge, historical amnesia and intellectual authority: Deconstructing hegemony and the social and political implications of the curricular "other." In L. M. Semali, & J. L. Kincheloe (Eds.), *What is indigenous knowledge? Voices from the academy* (pp. 317–331). New York: Falmer Press.

Reagan, T. (2005). *Non-Western educational traditions: Indigenous approaches to educational thought and practice* (3rd Ed.), Mahwah, NJ: Lawrence Erlbaum Associates, Publishers.

Samovar, L. A., & Porter, R. E. (1991). *Communication between cultures.* Belmont, CA: Wadsworth Publishing Co.

Semali, L. M., & Kincheloe, J. L. (1999). Introduction: What is indigenous knowledge and why should we study it? In L. M. Semali & J. L. Kincheloe (Eds.), *What is indigenous knowledge? Voices from the academy* (pp. 3–57). New York: Falmer Press.

Wang, H. (2006a). *How cultural values shape Chinese students' learning experience in American universities.* Unpublished doctoral dissertation. The University of Georgia, Athens, GA.

Wang, H. (2006b). Teaching Asian students online: What matters and why? *PAACE Journal of Lifelong Learning, 15*, 69–84

West, D. A.(1996). Prologue. In S. O'Meara, & D. A. West (Eds.),

From our eyes: Learning from indigenous peoples (pp.1–12). Toronto: Garamond Press.

Wildcat, D. R. (2001). Indigenizing politics and ethics: A realist theory. In V. Deloria, Jr. & D. Wildcat, *Power and place: Indian education in America* (pp. 87–99). Golden, Colorado: American Indian Graduate Center and Fulcrum Resources.

CHAPTER 2

Islam's Lifelong Learning Mandate

Mazalan Kamis and Mazanah Muhammad

The chapter deliberates on adult learning viewed from Islamic lenses. The examination starts with looking at Islam not only as a religion but as a way of life for Muslims. This follows with the importance and purpose of knowledge and learning in Islam. Next the discussion moves on to two aspects of learning; the student-teacher dynamic and methodology. The last part of the chapter focuses on the chapter's central theme, adult learning as a lifelong agenda.

ISLAM AS A COMPREHENSIVE WAY OF LIFE

Islam is a monotheistic religion believing in the One God—which is known in Arabic as Allah. The word *Islam* originates from three Arabic letters (Sim, Lam, Mim) making the root word which means "to be in peaceful submission; to surrender; to obey; peace." From the religious context Islam means "total submission to the will of God and obedient to His law." The follower of Islam is called Muslim which is defined as one who strives to submit to the total will of God. From this very meaning for the faithful Muslims, Islam is not just a religion but a comprehensive way of life.

Reflecting on this notion, the founder of the religion, the Prophet of Islam, Muhammad—an illiterate Arabian trader—has shown that he was "more than just a religious figure, he was the catalyst for a revolution in politics, economics, law, and civilization" (Emerick, 2002, p. iv). According to Islamic tradition, Muhammad, the final prophet of God who proclaimed Islam in the seventh century, over a period of 23 years received a series of God's revelations through the angel Gabriel. The revelations were recorded into written form by his companions and then compiled into the Muslim Holy Book, the Qur'an.

From the first word revealed by God to Muhammad that is *Iqra* meaning "read," to the name *Qur'an* which means "The Reading," it is a well-accepted notion among Muslims that knowledge and the pursuit of knowledge or learning are of paramount importance to Islam. In almost all the Qur'an's 114 chapters, the concern for education, knowledge, and learning is mentioned. As evidenced in the Qur'an, Islam guides every facet of a Muslim's life from the moment one is born until the day one departs from this world. In this respect, this chapter will show that seeking knowledge is a lifelong learning agenda ordained by Islam.

Although Islam originates in Arabia, Muslims are now found scattered all over the world with the greatest number in non-Arab countries. Muslims now are numbering well over 1 billion, making it the fastest growing religion in the world. It has been reported that in New York City alone there are over 600,000 Muslims from every imaginable ethnicity and language group with over 100 mosques within the five boroughs of the city (D'Agostino, 2003). Despite the enormity of its membership, little is known in the West about the beliefs and customs of the communities. Oftentimes, the little that is known is misunderstood or misrepresented by literature and popular press.

Muslims submit to the core belief of the religion (called the Pillars of Islam) but their practices and perspectives of Islam are often colored by their social, cultural, and geographical origin. For example, Malay communities which populate the Malay archipelago of Southeast Asia are often cited as an example of a Muslim society that permits relatively egalitarian relations between the sexes (Karim, 1988). On the other hand some Muslim communities in the Middle East are known to advocate strict separation of gender. The writers of this chapter, Malays from Malaysia who have had the experiences of attending both Eastern and Western educational systems, make no claim that what are presented here characterize the ultimate explanation of an Islamic view on knowledge/learning, but rather the discussions reflect their perspectives and understanding of the subject as Malay Muslims from Malaysia.

ATTENTION TO LEARNING/ KNOWLEDGE SEEKING

Islam treats knowledge and learning as of paramount importance (Hague, 2004; Albertini, 2003). Islamic scholarly tradition throughout the centuries "has stressed the centrality of knowledge in Islam in the strongest terms" (Albertini, 2003, p. 458). The tradition follows injunctions derived from two of the most revered scriptural sources of knowledge in Islam, the Qur'an and Hadith. Muslims belief that the Qur'an is made up of literal Words of God revealed to Muhammad, and the Hadith is a collection of recording of the illustrious sayings and deeds of Muhammad (Emerick, 2002; Bulliet, 2004). Both sources which contain numerous passages exhorting believers to indulge in learning describe the nature of knowledge as taken to encompass broadly as "all there is to know" (Albertini, 2003, p. 457), be it of sacred or secular, methaphysical or physical, or theoretical or practical. *Sahih Al-Bukhari*, a series of Hadith compilations treated as highly reliable by Muslims, has more than 130 sayings emphasizing the high status of knowledge in Islam. According to Haque (2004), Al-Ghazzali, the prolific and well-known Islamic thinker, also considered as "the architect of the latter development of Islam" (p. 366), wrote an entire book on *Kitab al-Ilm* (The Book of Knowledge) in the 11th century. Al-Ghazzali, who drew from both the Qur'an and Hadith, wrote the book as part of his famous 40 books of *Ihya Ulum ad Din* (Revivification of Religious Sciences) (Albertini, 2005; Highland, 2004). In total, he wrote nearly 70 books.

For Muslims, the first revelation received by Muhammad from God attests clearly to the fact that learning is of utmost importance:

Read! In the name of your Lord, Who has created (all that exists). Read! And your Lord is the most generous. Who has taught (the writing) by the pen, has taught man that which he knew not. (Qur'an 96:1–5)

Scholarly narratives of the above event indicate that the revelation occurred during one day when Muhammad was in solitary retreat in a cave in Mecca—an act which he often indulged in during the later years prior to his Prophethood—when an intense supernatural experience happened to him. Emerick (2002) vividly described this incident in his book, *Muhammad: Critical Lives*:

> He was sitting alone . . . , when a presence seemed to enter the cave. Muhammad startled to see a vision of light in the form of a man standing before him, holding a scroll. "Read," the strange apparition commanded him. Muhammad, his lips trembling, honestly replied, "I can't read." The being spread his arms around Muhammad, who could not resist, and squeezed him in a numbing embrace that took the breath out of him. "Read," the being repeated. Muhammad, reeling from the embrace, protested, "But, I can't read!" Again the being embraced him . . . until Muhammad's lungs felt like they were about to burst. "Read," the voice . . . ordered gravely. Muhammad, not wanting to undergo another crushing embrace, snapped, "What should I read?" . . . [the] being recited, in melodious Arabic verses . . . Muhammad repeated these cryptic words several times until he had them memorized. (p. 57)

This incident had a far-reaching impact in symbolically shaping the Islamic worldview about knowledge and learning. To the Muslims, the fact that the first command God handed down to an illiterate 40-year-old man is related to the acts of reading and writing suggest that learning and knowledge have to become a central theme in the teaching of Islam and the life of its followers. What this suggests is that in Islam a person is never too unintelligent to seek knowledge nor too old to embark on the journey of learning.

Subsequently, history has shown that because of such profound stress on the pursuit of knowledge by Islam, the early Islamic Empire that lasted for nearly 1000 years is credited with unsurpassed achievements in such diverse fields which include among others: geometry, astronomy, medicines, optics, physics, geography, and philosophy, in addition to comprehensive contributions in theosophy, philosophy, and encyclopedic compilations (Nasr, 1987). Education and knowledge were unrivalled and led to the Muslim Empire to become the center of world trade (Mehmet, 1997). The Empire, dotted with nearly 60 major centers of learning spanning from Baghdad in the East to Cordoba in the West, had brought significant impact to knowledge development in Europe and contributed greatly towards the Renaissance. Every traditional Islamic city possessed public and private libraries and some cities like Cordoba and Baghdad boasted of libraries with over 400,000 books. Such cities also had bookstores, some of which sold a large number of titles. Among the remarkable characteristics of the Empire, considering the benchmark of the day was

> the practice of ethnic and religious tolerance. Also remarkable were their social welfare systems, attempts at universal education and healthcare, and possibly most contentiously, their approach to women's equality issues. Around a thousand years before the so-called Enlightenment in the West began the move towards these features, they were part and parcel of early Islamic civilization. (Lovat, 2005, p. 43)

Sadly, the Crusades and later, the colonization of Muslim territories led to the decline in the growth of knowledge and learning endeavor among Muslims.

PURPOSE OF KNOWLEDGE AND LEARNING

In Islam, there are two major purposes of learning; the first purpose is to bring humankind closer to God, and the second is to bring humans closer to His creation or the society at large. Seeking knowledge for the sole purpose of worldly personal gain is abhorred by Islam. To understand why the individualistic pursuit of knowledge is detested one must first understand how Islam treats knowledge.

Bringing Humankind Closer to God

According to the Qur'an (57:9), God declares that "He is the One who sends to his servants manifest signs (proof, evidences, verses, lessons, revelations, etc.) that He may lead you from the depths of darkness into the light." The verse is evidence that from the Islamic perspective, all knowledge belongs to God, and the seeking of knowledge will ultimately lead one to Him. Seeking knowledge is likened to seeking God and since God is "the source of knowledge, by knowing more they (the believers) felt they were drawing near to God" (Husain & Ashraf, 1979, p. 11). In fact learning is treated as an act of worship. The Qur'an declares that "Only those who have knowledge are the persons who know Allah well" (35:28). The implication is that "without knowledge one cannot know God and without God there is no true knowledge" (Hilgendorf, 2003, p. 64). That's why from a believer's perspective, the more learned one is the more pious one becomes because one is drawn closer to God. Subsequently, the closer one is drawn to God the more humble one becomes as one feels awed by His Greatness. As such, there is no room for an individualistic purpose of learning.

The Malays possess a similar concept within their cultural context which is clearly reflected in the famous *pribahasa* (proverb) *"Ikutlah resmi padi semakin berisi semakin tunduk"* (Follow the example of the rice plant, the more mature its seeds become, the further its branch (stalk) bends down). Being a peaceful and polite race the Malays thrive in using *pribahasa* to avoid confrontation during argumentation and to explain their worldview (Lim, 2002). They often used rice, a highly respected crop of the agrarian Malays of the yesteryears, to describe what the community views as goodness. Thus, the metaphorical presentation of the learned as having the quality of a rice plant in the above *pribahasa* reflects, first, the high regard the Malays have for people who are knowledgeable, and second, their expectation that the learned must always humble themselves.

In Islam, what distinguishes between people in the eyes of God is not wealth, gender, or color of their skin but rather how knowledgeable (pious) they are. The Qur'an declares that those who are knowledgeable are placed on a higher rank in the eyes of God; but their ranking depends on the beneficial effect that people can draw from them. According to Emerick (2002), Muhammad in his last sermon to his followers days before he passed away declares:

> All you belong to the line of Adam, and Adam was created from dust. An Arab is not better than a non-Arab nor is a white better than a black or a black better than a white except in piety. The noblest among you all is the one who is most pious. (p. 286)

This declaration clearly stresses to the believers that people are created equal but their knowledge makes them nobler. In fact, the Qur'an rhetorically asks "Are those who know equal to those who do not know?" (39:9). This is further supported by several more verses like "Allah will raise up to (suitable) ranks (and degrees) those of you who believe and who have been granted knowledge" (58:11).

Bringing Humankind Closer to Society

With the acquisition of knowledge, a person is duty bound to do something about it, and the failure to do so will incur the wrath of God. Once knowledge is acquired by an individual, it is obligatory for him/her to spread it as far away as possible (Qur'an, 3:184). Thus, one is duty bound to act upon the knowledge accordingly and is responsible to guide others towards goodness. Knowledge and learning are good only if "they serve to engender virtue in the individual and elevate the whole community" (Cook, 1999, p. 349). Both learners and society at large must benefit from knowledge acquisition. According to Hassan (1996), the Qur'an is filled with numerous verses that uphold the many "rights" espoused for the creation of a just society and its perspective drives the point that knowledge is a prerequisite for the creation of a just world in which authentic peace can prevail. Unfortunately, the trampling of human rights that prevail in many Islamic nations of today only shows that they fail to fully adhere to the doctrines espoused by the Qur'an. Such scenarios help to solidify negative stereotyping about Muslims and Islam, a view that was already prevalent in the West ever since the Crusades more than 10 centuries ago.

Al Attas (1977), echoing similar ideas about knowledge brought about by numerous Islamic thinkers, noted that there is no dichotomy between worldly and heavenly knowledge since all knowledge belongs and leads to God. However, he stresses that in Islam knowledge can be hierarchically divided in two: Fard 'Ain (revealed knowledge), and Fard Kifayah (acquired knowledge). The two kinds of knowledge share unity of purpose to molding humans to be capable of maintaining prosperity on earth. Fard 'Ain is obligatory for every individual Muslim to acquire which most often focuses on learning about the ritualistic aspects of the religion, while Fard Kifayah is not obligatory upon individuals but rather upon Muslim communities and relates to communal interests. This emphasis on a communal learning obligation is unique as it stresses the believers' responsibility to society. For example, Fard Kifayah stipulates that if there is no medical doctor to serve a community, then it is obligatory upon the community to send one or more of its members for medical training, and failure to do so will result in each member sharing the community sin. What we can deduce here is that an ideal Islamic community can be described as one that is wholesomely self-sustaining and robustly involved in learning. Mehmet (1997) noted that Al-Ghazzali—the famous Islamic scholar who has been cited in the second subsection of this chapter—focused on the development of the individual Muslim whom he describes as "individual-in-community" (p. 1205). Such an individual is portrayed as an

> individual with a spiritual as well as a social personality. Spirituality gave the individual inner strength . . . The individual's social and material needs enable complete living . . . but their satisfaction demanded moderation and avoidance of access. Respect

for and tolerance of others were essential requisites of virtuous living . . . Here, individual identity is a multilayered manifestation, expanding and developing from the self through self in family, then in neighborhood, and finally in Ummah, the global brotherhood of the faithful. (p. 1205)

Clearly, this notion of individual contrasts rather sharply with the individualism espoused by the West, for, Mehmet (1997) stresses that in Islam "In all actions, personal, economic, social and political, the individual must be guided by rights and duties to God and others in interpersonal relations. Sharing, reciprocity and charity are essential requirements in demonstrating virtue" (p. 1205). The individual must "internalize community preferences as a responsible member of society . . . " (p. 1206) and turn away from the world of "selfish desires" (Highland, 2004, p. 261).

ROLE AND ETIQUETTE IN STUDENT-TEACHER RELATIONS

Islam recognizes that learning and teaching are equally important as both are directed to realize the greatness of God. In his last sermon the Prophet is reported to have said "Let those who are present inform those who are not." In another hadith, the Prophet calls for a person to "be a scholar/teacher . . . , or be a student who studies, or be a listener who listens to people who teach. Do not fall into the fourth category i.e. hater of the above." Even Muhammad declares himself "Verily! I was not sent but as a teacher." The discussion has shown that the Islamic notion of education integrates the rational, spiritual, and social dimensions of a person (Cook, 1999) and is crucial as both religious and social duty (Lovat, 2005). This concept is grounded on sincerity where knowledge gained is meant to guide practice and espouse humility. In another hadith the Prophet is reported to have declared that "Actions are but by intention and every man shall have but that which he intended."

Just as the Prophet is venerated in the Islamic tradition, the position of a teacher is revered in a society for that person is following in the footsteps of the Prophet for becoming a keeper of God's treasure; that is, knowledge. This position is strengthened by a proclamation by Muhammad "Verily the men of knowledge are the inheritors of the prophets." In Islam, the teacher is like the sun, which being itself luminous, sheds light; so venerated is such a person that according to Faris and Ashraf (2003), in their translation of Al-Ghazzali's *Kitab al-Ilm*, noted that in Islam, the passing away of a whole tribe is more tolerable than the death of one learned man. The student-teacher relationship is thus sacred. Therefore, the student is expected to observe *adab* (proper conduct) when interacting with the teacher.

The concept of *adab* is derived from the medieval Persian-Islamic world and has complex and multifaceted meaning that refers to the discipline of body, mind, and spirit which can be loosely described as "an outward expression of one's relation to God" (Loewen, 2003, p. 550). *Adab* is strictly observed by those who follow the mystical Sufic tradition, the kind of Islam that was brought to the Malay Archipelago. According to Harun (2004), quoting from an old manuscript of a dictionary on Islam, *adab* may be defined as "discipline of the mind and manners, good education and good breeding, polite deportment, a mode of conduct or behavior" (p. 24). To the Malays, observing the *adab* would ensure that the knowledge gathered by the student is a *baraka* (blessing) from God. *Adab* is treated more as proper outer conduct than as a mark of inner conduct. Among the acts of *adab* practiced by this chapter's authors as young Malay students were avoiding walking in front of their teachers, walking with a slight bow when they had to walk past or in front of their teachers, and kissing the hand of their teachers when shaking hands with them. All these and many other proper outward behaviors were practiced by the writers as a mark of respect to their teachers.

LEARNING METHODOLOGY

There are several methodologies of learning that are prevalent within the Islamic tradition. According to Haque (2004),

Al-Ghazzali—the famous Islamic "philosopher, theologian, jurist, and mystic" (p. 366)—suggests several methods of learning namely: imitation, logical reasoning, contemplation, and/or intuition. For the purpose of this book, we decided to focus on four methodologies which also encompass the classification by Al-Ghazzali. The four are memorization, knowledge circle, modeling, and reflection. The following paragraphs briefly describe each method.

Memorization

Memorization has been an important learning methodology for many religions including early Islam. Throughout his 23 years of Prophethood, Muhammad received revelations which he commanded his early followers to memorize and scribble on numerous object such as papyrus, leather, stone, and wood (Emerick, 2003). Muslims are encouraged to memorize the verses, and the reading of the Book itself is considered an act of worship (Robinson, 1996). Muslims must memorize certain chapters of the Qur'an in order to perform the compulsory five daily prayers, which make up one of the Pillars of the religion. In Malaysia, children are taught to read and memorize the Qur'an at a very early age, typically before they start formal schooling. Unlike other books, the reading and memorization must follow a very rigid system of classical Qur'anic Arabic and often takes years to master.

Knowledge Circle

During his early years as a Prophet, Muhammad faced great hostilities from the tribes of Mecca. He was not allowed to teach in the open and instead carried his teaching among his closest companions who often sat in circle listening to and discussing matters with him (Emerick, 2003). This is known as *Halaqa* or knowledge circle and it is a popular learning methodology among Muslims. The method gained new ground in the

1960s and 1970s when many Muslim nations gained independence from colonial powers which led to the opening of new doors for the revival of Islam among the nations' populations.

Modeling

The prophet is the best model for every Muslim. Every move he made and everything he said were recorded as his *Sunnah* by people close to him, which was then compiled into books of Hadith. So, Muslims learn how to live their life by imitating how the prophet reportedly conducted his life. One major example is the hajj, the ritual of pilgrimage to Mecca, which is also one of the five Pillars of Islam. During the final year of his life, the prophet instructed thousands of his followers to follow him from Medina to Mecca so that he can show them how to perform the ritual correctly (Emerick, 2002). The Prophet died soon after the hajj after he had pronounced that God's revelation was then complete. Throughout the 23 years of his teaching, history has proven that Muhammad, through his words and his actions, had successfully tamed the behaviors of Arabian tribes known for the hardness of their heart (Emerick, 2002; Saritoprak, 2005).

Reflection

Muslims believe that God guides humans through His Word in the Qur'an to investigate the phenomena of nature, so that they would recognize, worship, and serve Him. The text of the Qur'an is replete with verses inviting people to use their intellect, to ponder, to think, to know, and to marvel of His creation, for the goal of human life is to discover the Truth which is none other than worshipping God in His Oneness. For example, the Qur'an suggests that humankind contemplate on why God created diversity, "O Humanity, We created you from a single pair of male and female and made you into nations and tribes so you can come to know each other" (49:13). In numer-

ous other verses of the Qur'an, humans are asked to travel the
world so they can better reflect on their actions (3:137; 6:11;
16, 36).

LEARNING AS A LIFELONG ENDEAVOR

From the translation of Al-Ghazzali's celebrated work *Kitab
al-Ilm* by Faris and Ashraf (2003) one can see that, in Islam, the
pursuit of knowledge and learning should be a lifelong endeavor
as well as humanity's truest accomplishment. The next three
subtopics discuss the elements that support this notion.

Cradle-to-Grave Ethos

Learning is a lifelong endeavor in Islam as reflected by the
famous saying of Muhammad, "Seek knowledge from the cradle
to the grave." This saying is taken by Muslim parents as an injunction to place a child on a learning path very early in life;
that is immediately after being born. According to Islamic tradition, when a baby is born, he or she will be given to an adult,
preferably the father, who will whisper to the baby's ear the
Muslim call to prayer. The significance of this act is that the first
thing a baby hears and thus learns is concerned with the appreciation of the greatness of God. According to tradition, when
a baby is born, the child is like a clean pure-white sheet, and it
is the parents who are responsible in painting it. Malay parents are always reminded about the need to institute learning
early in the life of their children which is reflected by an age old
pribahasa: Meluntur buluh biarlah dari rebung (To bend a bam-
boo, one must start when it was still a shoot). A famous traditional lullaby sang by Malay parents to their children reads *Buai
laju-laju sampai cucur atap, belum tumbuh gigi sudah pandai
baca kitab* (Rock the swing to reach the cornice of a roof, yet to
start teething but already started reading).

If learning starts immediately after birth, when does it
end? Muslims believe that God's knowledge is infinitely vast as

such, like a drop of water in the sea; one can never complete acquiring it—a notion supported by the Qur'an (18:109). In other words, from an Islamic perspective, only death can stop one from learning. True to its call for continuous learning, Islam taught its believers to profess to the Oneness of God even when they are already on their deathbed. The last thing that a person can give to a dying family member is teaching the *shahadah* by whispering to his or her ear. The *shahadah*— professing the oneness of God, and testifying that Muhammad is His Messenger—is part of the call to prayer. As explained in the previous paragraph, the same call is whispered to a newborn. In Islam, learning truly starts from the cradle and only ends at the grave.

Setting a leading example, Muhammad, despite being the most knowledgeable and the most pious, shows that he still needs to continue learning as reflected in his famous prayers "O God, grant me knowledge of the ultimate nature of things." Here, knowledge or *ilm* in Arabic, in absolute sense is the one that opens the mind and souls to the supremacy of God. So, it is of little surprise when the Qur'an exhorts the believers to pray for the advancement in knowledge (20:114). In the village where the authors come from, learning activities conducted at the village's mosque, *madrassa*, and community hall continue to be actively carried out today. There are both formal and nonformal classes for men, women, youth, and children. A study on learning in community in Malaysia found that learning activities within both rural and urban communities are still very robust (Muhammad & Mat Junoh, 2003). Though the topics being presented are normally religious in nature, presenters often move into other subject matters of interest to the attendees.

Borderless Learning

So important is knowledge and learning, the Qur'an commands Muslims not to neglect them even during the time of war as indicated by verses from the Holy Book:

With all this, it is not desirable that all believers take to the field (in the time of war). From within every group in their midst some shall refrain from going to war, and shall devote themselves (instead) to acquiring a deeper knowledge of the Faith, and (thus be able to) pass their knowledge to their home-coming brethren, so that these (too) might guard themselves against evil. (9: 122)

The learning needs of the community must always be cared for, even during time of great crisis. The first author conducted qualitative research to find evidence of transformative learning among Malay professionals during the economic and political uncertainties in Malaysia in the late 1990s. He found that although many respondents believed in the need to participate in street protests, they also understood the need for well-educated professionals like themselves to restrict their involvement in such protests in order to develop new strategies that could enhance their political causes (Kamis, 2002). If learning is being stressed even in the time of war, it is even more so in the time of peace.

There is little surprise now if people go in droves in search of new knowledge and wealth in China since the country is rapidly growing and one day may surpass the United States in its economic superiority. In the seventh century, the Chinese Empire was indeed extremely remote from Arabia, but even then Muhammad encouraged Muslims to "go in search of it [knowledge] as far as China" (Siddiqui, 2003, p.1), proving that one should seek learning opportunities wherever they may be and in the process strive to overcome barriers to learning, which in this case was geographical. What was literal then proves to be very visionary indeed, as the call also prompts the expansion of Islam beyond Arabia into Central Asia.

The need for expanding the horizon to learn is evidenced in the Qur'an (29:20) "Travel through the earth and see how Allah originates creation." The exhortation to travel the world in search of knowledge is reflected by various types of travel familiar to many Muslims, all of which may entail both physical movement and spiritual transformation. Among them include the *hajj* (pilgrimage to Mecca), *hijra* (emigration), *rihla* (travel in pursuit of knowledge), and *ziarah* (visits to the sick/shrines).

Any single journey may include all four of the purposes. Muslims are being taught that the journey that one takes to indulge in learning, be it literal or otherwise, is a way to Paradise. This is reflected by a hadith where Muhammad is reported to have said to his followers:

> God makes the path to paradise for him who travels a road in search of knowledge, and the angels spread their wings for the pleasure of the seeker of knowledge. All those in heaven and earth will seek forgiveness from those who pursue knowledge. . . . The learned person is superior to the worshipper just as the moon has precedence over the rest of the stars.

Every act undertaken in one's learning endeavor is considered an act of worship, a fact that can be deducted in another saying of Muhammad, that, "even the sleep of a person in pursuit of learning is regarded as worship" if the sleep is to make him fresh again to seek knowledge.

Democratization of Knowledge and Learning

According to Emerick (2002), because of the moral and social obligation associated with knowledge and learning, Muhammad is reported to have made a declaration that the acquisition of knowledge is incumbent upon all Muslims regardless of their gender. Such a declaration may sound mundane in the world of today, but in the seventh century Arabia where the customs had always dictated that women should take no role in public activities, the call must have generated considerable uproar for it was calling for equal right of access to knowledge and learning regardless of gender. Muhammad brings the message that men and women were equal in the sight of God as stated in the Holy Book:

> Lo! Men who surrender unto Allah, and women who surrender, and men who believe and women who believe, and men who obey and women who obey, and men who speak the truth and women who speak the truth, and men who persevere (in righteousness) and women who persevere, and men who are humble

and women who are humble, and men who give alms and women who give alms, and men who fast and women who fast, and men who guard their modesty and women who guard (their modesty), and men who remember Allah much and women who remember—Allah hath prepared for them forgiveness and a vast reward. (33:35)

Sadly, some so-called Muslim communities have been known to forbid their female populace from schooling or have access to certain fields of knowledge, an injunction that runs counter to the message brought by Islam. Though this is not widespread, it has helped to demonize Islam in the eyes of the world. However, for a country like Malaysia, where progressive approaches to Islam have been in practice, men and women, Muslim and non-Muslim alike, continue to enjoy equal access to knowledge and learning. Much like the experience of the authors of this paper, who are of different genders and hail from different parts of the country, the doors to learning have been equally open for them to indulge in all manner and types of learning.

CONCLUSION

Learning is truly a lifelong endeavor where age, socioeconomic status, gender, geography, and race must never be allowed to become barriers. In some aspects, an Islamic perspective on learning differs from the West. This includes the purpose of knowledge, communal obligation, responsibility to share knowledge, and the teacher-student relationship. Islam has indeed highlighted the simple fact that to live a blessed and successful life in this world, one must have and continue to acquire knowledge.

REFERENCES

Al-Attas, S. M. N. (1977). *Aims and objectives of Islamic education.* London: Hodder and Stoughton.

Albertini, T. (2003). The seductiveness of certainty: The destruction of Islam's intellectual legacy by the fundamentalists. *Philosophy East & West*. 53 (4) 455–470. University of Hawai'i Press.

Albertini, T. (2005). Crisis and certainty of knowledge in Al-Ghazzali (1058–1111) and Descartes (1596–1650). *Philosophy East & West*. 55(1) 1–14. University Hawai'I Press.

Birke, L. & Whitworh, R. (1998). Seeking knowledge: Women, science and Islam. *Women's Science International Forum*. 21(2) 147–159. Elsevier Science Ltd.

Bulliet, R. W. (2004). *The case for Islamo-Christian civilization*. New York: Columbia University Press.

Coles, M. I. (2004). Education and Islam: A new strategic approach. *Race Equality Teaching*, 22(3), 41–46.

Cook, B. J. (1999). Islam versus western conception of education: Reflections on Egypt. *International Review of Education*. 45 (3/4) 339–357.

D'agostino, M. (2003). Muslim personhood: Translation, transationalism and Islamic religious education among Muslims in New York City. *Journal of Muslim Minority Affairs*. Vol 23 (2) 285–294.

Emerick, Y. (2002). *Muhammad: Critical lives*. Alpha Books: Indianapolis.

Faris, N. A. & Ashraf, S.M (2003). *The Book of knowledge: Being a translation with notes of Kitab al-'Ilm of Al-Ghazzalis's Ihya' 'Ulum al-Din*. Online edition http://www.ghazali.org/works/bk1-sec-1.htm Access 9/8/2004.

Hague, A. (2004). Psychology from the Islamic perspective: Contributions of early Muslim scholars and the challenges to contemporary Muslim psychologists. *Journal of Religion and Health* 43 (4) Winter. 357–377. Blanton-Peale Institute.

Harun, J. (2004). Bustan Al-Salatin, 'The garden of kings': A universal history and Adab work from seventeenth-century Aceh. *Indonesia and the Malays World*. 32(92) 21–52. Carfax Publishing.

Hassan, R. (1996). Religious human rights in the Qur'an. In John Witte, Jr. & Johan Van der Vyver (Eds.), *Religious human rights in global perspective: Religious perspectives* (361–86).

Hellmich, C. (2005). Al-Qaeda-terrorists, hypocrites, fundamentalists? The view from within. *Third World Quarterly*. 26(1) 39–54. Routledge.

Highland, J. (2004) The thought of Al-Ghazzali and Symeon: Guidance, tolerance, and the reverent mindset in the thought of Al-Ghazzali and Symeon. *The Muslim World*. 94. April. 259–273.

Hilgendorf, E. (2003). Islamic education: History and tendency. *Peabody Journal of Education*, 78(2), 63–75. Lawrence Erlbaum Associates, Inc.

Husain, S. S. & Ashraf, S. A. (1979). *Crisis in Muslim education*. London: Hodder and Stoughton.

Kamis, M. (2002). *Transformative learning among educated young Malay professionals*. Unpublished doctoral thesis. Universiti Putra Malaysia.

Karim, W. (1988). Women's contribution to culture: Malay women in Adat and Islam, in Aihwa Ong (1990) State versus Islam: Malay families, women's bodies, and the body politic in Malaysia. *American Ethnologist*. 17(2) May, 258–276. American Anthropological Association.

Lim, K. H. (2002). Budi *as the Malay mind: A philosophical study of Malay ways of reasoning and emotion in* Peribahasa. Unpublished doctoral dissertation: University of Hamburg.

Khan, M. M. (Translator) (1994). *The translation of the meaning of English*. Riyadh-Saudi Arabia: Maktaba Dar-us-Salam Publications.

Khan, M. M., & Al-Hilali, M. T. (1995). *Interpretation of the meanings of the noble Qur'an in the English language* (12th ed.). Riyadh-Saudi Arabia: Dar-us-Salam Publications.

Loewen, A. (2003). Proper conduct (Adab) is everything: The Futuwwat-namah-I Sultani of Hussyn Va'is-I Kashifi. *Iranian Studies*. 36 (4) Dec. Carfax Publishing.

Lovat, T. J. (2005). Educating about Islam and learning about self: An approach for our times. *Religious Education*. 100 (1) 38–51. Winter. The Religious Education Association

The Meaning of the Glorious Qur'an (M. Pikthall, Trans.) (1999). Retrieved October 13, 2006, from http://www.al-sunnah.com/cal_to_islam/quran/pickthall

Mehmet, O. (1997). Al-Ghazzali on social justice: Guidelines for a new world order from an early medieval scholar. *International Journal of Social Economics*. 24 (11), 1203—1218. MCB University Press.

Muhammad, M., & Junoh, A. M. (2003). Community based adult learning in Malaysia. In M. Osborne & V. Gallacher (Eds.) *Experiential: Community: Workbased: Researching learning outside the Academy*. Proceedings of Researching Widening Access: International Perspectives Conference (pp. 277–287). The Centre for Research in Life Long Learning, Glasgow Caledonian University, Glasgow, Scotland.

Nasr, S. H. (1987). *Traditional Islam in the modern world*. London: KPI Limited.

Pridmore, S., & Pasha, M. I. (2004) Psychiatry and Islam. *Australasian Psychiatry*. 12(4) 380–385. December.

Robinson, N. (1996). *Discovering the Qur'an: A contemporary approach to a veiled text*. London: SCM Press Ltd.

Saidul Islam, M. (2005). Muslims in the capitalist discourse: Sept 11 and its aftermath. *Journal of Muslim Minority Affairs*. 25 (1) 3–12 April. Routledge.

Saritoprak, Z. (2005). An Islamic approach to peace and non-violence: A Turkish experience. *The Muslim Journal, 95*(3), 413–427.

Siddiqui, B. H. (2003) Knowledge: An Islamic perspective. *Cultural Heritage and Contemporary Change Series* IIA (3) Online journal available at http://www.crvp.org/book/Series02/IIA-3/. Access on 1/31/2006.

Underwood, S. M., Shaikha, L., & Bakr, D. (1999). Veiled yet vulnerable: Breast cancer screening and the Muslim way of life. *Cancer Practice* 7(6) 285–290. American Cancer Society.

CHAPTER 3

American Indian Indigenous Pedagogy

Paula Gunn Allen

> I will tell you something about the stories,
> [he said]
> They aren't just entertainment.
> Don't be fooled.
> They are all we have, you see,
> all we have to fight off
> illness and death.
>
> You don't have anything
> if you don't have the stories. . . . "
> —Leslie Marmon Silko
> *Ceremony*

Since time immemorial humans have explored ways of transmitting knowledge to their young. Devising a variety of ways over the millennia, various cultures have developed methodologies that suit the adult that they hopefully assume the child or children being raised will become.

Those tribal methods that are still extant (as well as those earlier ones we know little or nothing about) share with all other methods the goal of making each child able to function effectively in the community as an adult. Once tribal knowledge centered on such matters as hunting, gathering, and horticulture, constructing housing of either the temporary or permanent sort, and participating in various religious and cultural events, and traditional methodology was aimed at developing adeptness in neophytes. The methodology has changed little, although the "subjects" have changed considerably.

As I was growing up my mother taught me things without teaching them directly. Her method is commonly used by modern Native people, even those who believe they know little or nothing of their own nation's tradition. Seldom does an adult directly instruct a child. Instead, they do what I came to see as "talking around the edges," combined with the "show it don't say it" method. This strategy can be applied in various ways. One is by talking about something pertinent to the child's education with another person or persons in the presence of the child. It is assumed, usually rightly, that the child will "overhear."

Another application, which is among non-Natives the one most likely to be identified as "Indian pedagogy," is storytelling. Storytelling is the formal method of indirect teaching. Its efficacy depends on being accompanied by consistent behavior on the part of the significant adults in the child's world as well as on its pertinence to the child's situation or concerns of the moment. Traditionally, stories are often chosen because they speak to something of immediate concern to the child and/or to the adults concerned with the child's upbringing.

In the contemporary educational system, there have been a few education projects focused on developing materials that speak to the background and experiences of many Native children—particularly those raised in rural and/or reservation settings. In some cases, they have brought storytellers from nearby Native communities into the classroom. Alternatively, they have also made use of published materials, some developed by tribal educators, many taken from sources far from Indian country, but seen as "Indian" stories nonetheless. While this approach at least recognizes the wisdom of suiting the education to the student, it leaves much to be desired.

The problem with this approach in the classroom is that the stories chosen in a family setting are selected for appropriateness for a given child or situation, in the real world, the one the child lives in, while curricular choices don't have that luxury.

Stories that are used as artifacts of a culture otherwise invisible to and within the educational system are as likely to instruct Indian and non-Indian children alike how to discount Indian ideas while seemingly privileging them. This result is likely because the stories sound incomplete or exotic when ripped from the context of daily life.

My mother used the tribal method in raising us, and I am pretty certain she would never have perceived or characterized her style as "Indian." It was how one raised children, she must have felt, probably because her mother had done something similar raising my mother, and so on all the way back for centuries. Of course, being a compulsive reader she used printed materials. She made her choices on the basis of their "literary" value, choosing selections from Mother Goose, the King James version of the Bible, Aesop's Fables, Laguna folk tales, Grimm's fairy tales, Rudyard Kipling, and dozens of other sources.

But beyond reading to us and sometimes reciting things like:

The gingham dog and the calico cat
Side by side on the table sat
'Twas half-past twelve and what do you think?
Nor one nor the other had slept a wink. . . .

Or "There once was a puffin who looked just like a muffin/And he lived at the bottom of the deep blue sea. . . . " or my all-time favorite, Hugh Mearn's succinct posing of how we know what is real and what is false:

As I was going up the stair
I met a man who wasn't there.
He wasn't there the other day;
I wish that man would go away.

These stories and poems enthralled me, making me as compulsive a reader as my mother, and generating in me a lifelong love affair with poetry, fiction, and tribal life and cultures, not to mention materials drawn from the oral tradition of my varied ancestry and those sources discovered in school or on somebody's shelf.

The thing about reading and/or telling or reciting to a

child or a group of children is that the message implied in the tale or poem is as important as its entertainment and social bonding value. (Wasn't it Aristotle who opined that the purpose of art was to delight, move, and entertain us—or was it Alexander Pope?) In Indian country the story must be accompanied with actions that bespeak its underlying meanings. My mother comes from a culture, Laguna Pueblo, that is conflict-phobic. She assumed, probably without being conscious of why she made that choice, that this poem and others such as the Puffin one, show that fighting, that is, conflict, is likely to result in disaster, while cooperating is likely to result in harmony and increased personal pleasure and satisfaction in terms of community as well as the individual's life.

So, what can one learn from the fight between the gingham dog and calico cat? I learned and continue to learn various things in addition to "fighting is so bad it can annihilate both of you." I learned that "inanimate objects" were neither, which nourished my imagination while providing me with insights into the workings of the universe that would serve me in good stead through my years as student then professor in educational institutions. I also learned that one of the outcomes of intense fighting was the annihilation of the warring parties. I learned that old folks are repositories of wisdom: not the kind that means words, words, words, as Eliza Doolittle so furiously laments in the musical, *My Fair Lady*.

The old Dutch Clock and the Chinese Plate had knowledge that enabled them to predict the future with perfect accuracy:

> The old Dutch Clock and the Chinese Plate
> Seemed to know as sure as Fate
> That there would be a terrible spat.

Not only did they know the likeliest outcome of the enmity between the gingham dog and the calico cat, but they could share their experience with another, the narrator of the poem. I liked that the narrator shifted: when mother read or recited the poem, she was the narrator who claimed "I wasn't there, I simply state/What was told to me/By the Chinese Plate." But when I was reciting, I became the confidant of the Chinese Plate's stories; I became the bearer of tradition. What I gleaned from mother's stories was not so much a conscious accumulation of information but guidance that has had lifelong consequences. For one thing, eventually I focused on writing and teaching literature, as my avocations; my vocation became finding and chatting with the Chinese Plate and its associates.

While I was learning to avoid conflict, thus being enculturated in Laguna super-pacifist values, I was also learning that harmony depended on recognizing that all beings have a place within the community and must be accorded respect, however curious according respect to "inanimate objects" might seem to those otherwise reared.

A more widespread dimension of "teaching around the edges," one that I believe occurs in most households, is the simple conversation I mentioned earlier. In this method family members might talk about the day's significant happenings at dinner, or they might make a running commentary on the shows or the commercials that run while they're watching television or videos. Their stories about their day inform the children about the greater world and how to perceive, act, and react within it, while the commentary offers information about how to view certain sources or structures, in this way upholding certain values and rejecting others. For instance there might be a program, a "sit-com," that takes up some social theme such as dating, marital spats, or the relation between the good guys and the bad guys. How to think about marital spats is in part influenced by the show itself . . . the dialogue, action, settings; in a sit-com they will all end up resolving the conflict and living happily ever after, or at least until next week's program. But to a greater extent the significance of conflict within a family and how to view and handle it is influenced by the family itself. This influence goes well beyond the comments made during a given viewing; talk that is either contradicted or reinforced by actual behavior will in large measure determine the child's perspective and eventual behavior in conflict circumstances.

As for the "good guys, bad guys" so embedded in U.S. American narratives, its influence is bone deep. When my nephew was around four years old he was playing with some plastic cowboys, all the same color. He began to tell me about the fight that was going on, his story emphasized by moving men around or having them bang on or against one another. The story was about the good guys doing this and that to the bad guys and vice-versa. As they were all the same color I asked he how he could tell the good guys from the bad guys. "Easy," he said. "The good guys kill the bad guys and the bad guys kill people." Wow. American politics at every level, so succinctly synopsized.

Conflict structure characterizes most television programs and commercials, as well as most popular fiction, comic books, and electronic, role-playing, and board games; that is, the Euro-American narrative tradition is based on that model. It is this conflict-based structure that shapes all its societal attitudes and institutional structures. When parents cheer the "good guy" and tacitly agree that the villain deserves what he or she "gets," they are teaching a significant lesson: that the inevitable collision of opposing forces, one socially and/or morally righteous and the other socially destructive and immoral, is a "fact." It is reality. It must be: our entire civilization is founded on it. Because this primal structure is present in every social institution—education, religion, government, even entertainment—it "proves" that conflict is an essential fact of life. Indeed, the two-party (or even multiple party) system, the bestowal of "grades" on learners that result in his or her ability to get the goodies modern life offers in adulthood, competitive sports and the society's enthrallment with them, the adversarial nature of lawsuits and criminal prosecutions, even the depiction of illness and healing, aging and death, are couched in the vocabulary of an evil force pitted against a good force.

I have tried to imagine such a society developing in Indian Country, and I find that I can't, although some contemporary trends make me wonder. The problem is, I believe, a matter of what basic (and largely unspoken) assumptions form the base of the society. One grounded in the principles of harmony, integrity, respect for all, and kinship is not likely to develop institutions based on conflict, hatred, separateness, isolation, or a "trust no one" approach to social interactions. Because the assumptions in the two paradigms differ so profoundly, it is little wonder that their pedagogies differ greatly as well.

For instance, suppose a child is having difficulty being respectful to others—family, friends, teachers, pets, field mice, snakes, whatever. The conversation at the supper table can be about how disrespectful some acquaintance has been on some occasion or another and the consequences of that disrespect. Of course, it helps if the consequences the offender suffered have meaning to the child beyond "time out," or "no ice cream for you tonight, buster." An Indian mother of my acquaintance recounted one of her moves to inculcate respect for others in her young son. He had wanted a hampster, which he had gotten. Soon enough, of course, the novelty wore off, and he put off cleaning the animal's cage until the stink was considerable, saying "I forgot," when his mother mentioned the smell. So, instead of cleaning it herself, thus teaching him that he didn't have to be responsible or respectful, or engaging in a power struggle with him, thus teaching him that escalating conflict is a good problem-solving strategy, she came up with a clever approach. She disabled the toilet her son used and kept "forgetting" to call the plumber. Soon enough the boy was complaining about the stench in his bathroom, and mom just nodded wisely. "Yep," she agreed at his complaints. "Do you think that might be just how your hamster feels?" The boy kept the cage clear, and mother reattached the flush mechanism on his toilet and life went on. With a difference: her child had learned a lesson that would stand not only him in good stead, but would in a small way benefit the community around him, including the environmental one.

It must be said that the deep-seated assumption that harmony, integrity, balance, and kinship are the fundamental characteristics of decently lived human life and of all that I am describing has a down side. While it sounds ideal, it leads to its own problems: mainly it sets the society that holds to it up for conquest by any conflict-based paradigm. Those who assume that harmony and balance are primary don't fight back, which, alas was the flip side of my mother's belief and teaching about how conflict was always ill-advised. In the 20th century when men from those Pueblos that were conflict-phobic went to war they were expected to undergo extensive ritual cleansing prior to returning to their home villages.

The idea was that men who had been drenched in conflict would inevitable bring the ugliness of war and anguished death home with them unless their spirits were returned to harmony. Two novels, Pulitzer Prize–winning *House Made of Dawn* by Kiowa writer N. Scott Momaday (1968), and *Ceremony* by Laguna writer Leslie Marmon Silko (1977), as well as some of the short stories in *The Man to Send Rain Clouds,* edited by Kenneth Rosen (1974), took up this theme. Each of the protagonists was in World War II, and the consequences of their service and the lack of healing rituals provided for them inform the works with a meaning that goes beyond war and death as it goes beyond "ethnic" literature. Each of these works in its way provides a deep insight into another way of being, another way of viewing conflict, another way of being human. "All we have are the stories." But more, if, as I have come to believe, we *are* the stories. For not only do the narratives of our societies form our own "personal" narratives and thus our personalities, characters, and destinies, but every individual within every narrative tradition (e.g., "society" or "community") is an analog of some character in that narrative tradition. I don't mean that we use characters from narratives we hear or see growing up. After all the tradition predates and postdates any individual's lifespan. It is, from a human point of view, ancient if not immortal. But the stories live through individuals as through human social systems. And they keep repeating, iteration after iteration; what changes remains the same. Given this, or the possibility that the idea has merit, education founded on stories, narrative structures drawn from varied traditions is inevitably the most effective mode.

Maybe that's why children learn so much more from media than from the classroom. "Just the facts, ma'am" can hardly excite a young, vital mind. And, in the interests of helping humans grow societies that are more nurturing than destructive, perhaps attention to narratives—those told and lived at home as well as those in media, educational and other official venues—can be a potent agent of social transformation.

The consequences that have significance, personal, experiential meaning to a child have a lot to do with the values and unspoken assumptions society holds. And these are embedded in its stories. There are few real consequences of not remembering the multiplication tables or the decimal system, at least not for many years. If one reads at a basic level, one can earn a decent living, eventually, but the "some day" scenario has little force over a child's day-to-day existence. Children tend to live in the here and now; adults in "civilized" societies hardly ever notice it.

One of the more important features of growing up Indian is the confusion dual identity causes in family and consequently in the growing child. Because the narrative traditions and the values and deep assumptions they dramatize differ so greatly, the conflict engendered in attempting to function within the differing parameters is tremendous. The highest teen suicide rate in the United States is that of Indian kids. The drop-out rate is huge, and the incidence of dysfunctional behaviors such as alcohol and drug abuse is great. The pervasiveness of the psychic suffering ocassioned a cliche about Native people who had for one reason or another been exposed too long to the non-Indian world; they were said to have "fallen between two chairs." Novels such as D'Arcy McNickle's *The Surrounded* or Joseph Mathews's *Sundown*, both written in the 1930s, took up the theme. Because they are built on a western conflict-based structure, the outcome for the protagonist cannot be good. Given that he comes into conflict with his dual identity because of the circumstances of his identity—both protagonists are mixed bloods—his fate is sealed; we know he will come to a bad end, and both do. In an earlier novel, *Cogewea, The Half-Blood*, written by Mourning Dove, Christine Quintasket, the protagonist, also a mixed blood, comes close to a bad end; however the pull of the old ways, symbolized by her grandmother, her innate strength, and the love of a good man, also a mixed blood, bring her through near death to a balanced life.

In general, American Indian communities have traditionally valued harmony, respect, integrity, and balance, both in terms of individual behavior and overall group dynamics. They have not valued conflict, competition based on conflict of interest or ego, or adversarialism as the foundations of society.

It is traumatic for contemporary Native people who hold to traditional values to navigate within the larger societies of the Americas. It's almost as difficult for those raised in a bicultural situation. After all, in every case the larger society is based on Western assumptions about the nature of reality and the place of humans within it. On the whole the Indo-European narrative tradition is based on conflict between good and evil as the fundamental trope, with the hero-savior narrative as its prime vehicle. This situation certainly brings the idea of conflict as a primary theme of life home to indigenous people; thus, the—not exactly new—situation requires some adjustment of traditional methods of educating the young. My mother developed some strategies of her own, based, I think, on her grandmother and mother's own educations in Indian Schools, which left them with information from two very different worlds and with what amounted to a command to resolve the effects of this "marriage." I was told by an old relative, Aunt Susie Marmon who was a bit younger than my great-grandmother, Meta Atseye Gunn, that Grandma Gunn was respected around the Pueblo for her ability to "walk in balance." That is, she took from each culture what was of use in a unified or integrated way, and made a life from her composition. Instead of perceiving the two cultures to be in conflict, she understood them (as all life) to be parts of a whole . . . maybe like the two wings of one bird which allow the creature to fly.

The most salient thing about "teaching around the edges," is that it rests almost entirely on showing how to function harmoniously and respectfully with integrity in what you do and the kind of person you are and you value, keeping a balance between traditional and modern ways.

What we have are the stories. After all, the stories contain and retain a point of view, a consciousness that has long characterized American Indians—and probably other tribal, land, and land-spirits-based peoples. The goal of educating the young in these kind of systems is to convey to them as Hamlet remarks "there are more things in heaven and earth, Horatio, than are dreamt of in your philosophies." No Indian-educated Indian could have said it better.

The other goal, entirely unstated and probably unnoticed, is that traditional educational systems, formal and informal, create a holistic mode of thinking\perception that must be integrated with experience. This in turn is exhibited in a variety of ways, "thinking—or talking—around the edges" being the most evident. But two others that spring to mind are witty humor—which is a fine survival trait—and a general noninvasive interpersonal style that characterizes both individuals and groups. As my mother phrased it, "mind your own business" was a rule. Briefly, this meant that what others did or believed was no one's business but their own. If one didn't share the other's values or care to participate in their activities, one didn't. But "carrying tales" or stirring up trouble because one disapproved was not on. Again, the idea here is that everything is connected to everything; or, as my mother taught me, "all life is a circle and everything has its place within it." I think she said that when I wanted to put a lizard I was holding in my pocket and she was explaining to me that lizards had their own ways and to let it be.

The concept, all life is a circle, that everything has a place within, is descriptive of the thesis that underlies Indian pedagogy. If everything is connected to everything, if there is no "hero," no object or event that is foregrounded, privileged, over and above others without good, temporary reason, then learning must proceed in a cumulative and connected manner. Thus information must be translated into experience, and the combination built on, extended, expanded, until the student's consciousness opens to grasp ever widening and deepening layers of comprehension and wisdom.

Teaching around the edges had its limits. On those occasions when some specific task such as using a sewing machine, driving a vehicle, preparing a certain dish, or repairing something like a car engine or washing machine motor is involved, direct instruction is necessary. In my experience the lessons didn't entail reading anything; whoever knew how to do the required task took you through it step by step then left you to it. They were of course assuming that you had been paying full attention to the instructions, would remember them in detail and proper sequence, and had enough sense to ask for help if attention had been faulty or memory failed. Most of all, this sort of instruction assumed the learner to be a capable being, an assumption that was not new but that had been threaded throughout the child's personal experience and in her or his observation of adult interactions. I recall a number of such lessons: one of the earliest was when I was around five. My mother finally agreed to allow me to do the dishes after I asked if I could for days—if not longer. After all, my older sisters got to do them all the time!

She set me up with a chair to stand on so I could reach the sink, filled the dishpan with warm soapy water, showed me how to rinse the soapy dishes and place them in the drainer. That done, she left me to it. What I remember most vividly was how huge the stack of dishes to be washed seemed, and how sorry I became that I had pestered to be allowed to wash them. I don't remember how it turned out. I imagine that one of my aunts, my father's younger sisters who were living with us at the time, may have come home from the store where they worked alongside my father and rescued me. Their approach to child rearing differed dramatically from my mother's, a fact which would cause confusion and tremendous emotional and intellectual conflict for me.

Leaving a child to discover on her own, through experience, the difference between reality and imagination was not a method they would have used. (Nor did they in rearing their own children.) However my dishwashing adventure ended, mother continued to rely on the old methods. I remember baking my first cake when I was seven. Mother gave me instructions, and helped me get the ingredients, mixing bowls and utensils together. Then she retired to the living room to read her book . . . a rare luxury for her in the middle of the day.

I didn't feel abandoned by her absence. I was sure I could bake a great chocolate cake by myself, and her confidence supported mine. Alas, the cake fell, and when dismayed I reported the sad outcome to mother she calmly commiserated, then showed me how to solve the problem by taking hunks of the cake and slathering an impromptu icing-pudding over the flat pieces. It tasted pretty good as I remember, and the family all agreed that they liked it.

Teaching around the edges has a variety of outcomes that function over the long term. One is that such teaching yields ever deepening layers of meaning over a lifetime. One meaning when first noticed at, say, 5 years of age turns into another meaning at 10, at 25, and at 60. It's as though an infinitely capacious bag of information, intelligence, and wisdom could spill out significances as needed forever. Neat. I have noticed this phenomena over the past 40 or 50 years, as well as that formal genres in the contemporary world, fiction, poetry, drama, film, and the like, have a similar effect. I have also noticed that some points made by a teacher, say in fifth grade or sophomore year of college hang on long after the utterance; indeed, long after whoever said it has died. Phrases like "Play it again, Sam," misquoted from *Casablanca* or "Beam me up, Scotty," from *Star Trek* take on a life of their own and inform both the conceptualization and imagination of generations to follow. Even Joe Friday's "Just the facts, ma'am," from 1950's television show *Dragnet*, is such an utterance and more so, summing up an entire culture's way of perceiving reality and functioning within it. For in the modern world facts are the thing. It is taken as a basic reality that such a thing as factuality exists, that life and the phenomena around us that make up our world can be measured, tested, and proven to exist.

A couple of years ago I was attending a meeting on "queer" Indians (or Two Spirits) held by the American Anthropology Association in San Francisco. One of the papers consisted of a Navajo man's experiences in learning the religions/spiritual tradition of his people at levels far beyond the usual. One thing he said struck a chord in me, and it was how the instructors went about teaching. They would instruct the young man in a certain ceremonial or background tradition, then send him off until further notice. He never knew how long it would be before the next session would be held; eventually he realized that his job was to live with the new information until it became knowledge. That is, just hearing about something, even when that hearing included a "hands-on workshop" was insufficient. A pupil must integrate himself and the information. Now, while everyday life and instruction, formal or informal, are not as demanding, nor do they hold the peril to self and others that walking the sacred ("shamanic") path does, the method is the same. Information, like the people being given it, must mature, or "get ripe." His story reminded me of a Laguna story about how humans were made.

When whatever "deity" it was made us—maybe Iyatiku, Beautiful Corn and her sister Sun Woman, she used corn meal she and her sister had ground. Mixing it with water they patted it into cakes then put them in the "beehive" oven traditionals still use to bake some of the best bread ever. They removed the first batch of cornbread too soon and it was too light. Determined to correct for that mistake with the second batch, they left it in too long, and it was too dark. The third batch, though, was a certain brown, and that was the one they chose to be us, the Lagunas, who, at least back then, before we became what I call "The Motley Clans," were varying shades of a coppery brown familiar to people everywhere as the "Indian" skin color. They chose it because, as she put it, "it was ripe." This story carries a weight of meanings, one being that we are made of corn (you are what you eat?) and corn is not only sacred it is the first four Clans of the People which are Red Corn, Blue Corn, Yellow Corn, and White Corn. Eventually another came into being, mixed-color corn which I think of as peculiarly American as well as Laguna, the Pueblo of motley.

In the tradition of American Indian civilization, the living beings and entire phenomena, or worlds if you like, that encompass them . . . and us . . . have an existence that is seen as real for all its immeasurable, unquantifiable nature. For us, myths are expressions of the nature of reality. We do not see them as fabrications constructed by people who were (and still are) too stupid (primitive) to get the facts, ma'am. The stories speak to and for an entire ancient civilization's way of perceiving reality and functioning within it. I must say it worked for thousands of years, so there might be something to it!

REFERENCES FOR FURTHER READING

Cajete, G. (1994). *Look to the mountain: An ecology of indigenous education*. Skyland, NC: Kivaki Press.

Deloria, V., Jr. (1995). *Red Earth, white lies: Native Americans and the myth of scientific fact*. New York: Scribner.

Deloria, V., Jr., & Wildcat, D. (2001). *Power and place: Indian education in America*. Golden, CO; Fulcrum Resources.

Gunn Allen, P. (1985). *The sacred hoop: Recovering the feminine in American Indian traditions*. Boston: Beacon Press.

Lame Deer, J., & Erdoes, R. (1972). *Lame Deer: Seeker of visions: The life of a Sioux medicine man*. New York: Simon and Schuster.

Linderman, F. B. (1932/1972). *Pretty shield: Medicine woman of the Crow*. New York: The John Day Company, 1932; rpt, University of Nebraska Press, 1972.

Mathews, Joseph. (1934). *Sundown*. New York: Longmans.

McNickle, D'Arcy. (1978/1935). *The surrounded*. Albuquerque: University of New Mexico Press.

Momaday, N. S. (1968). *House made of dawn*. New York: Harper & Row.

Momaday, N. S. (1969). *The way to rainy mountain*. Albuquerque: The University of New Mexico Press.

O'Meara, S., & West, D. A. (Eds.). (1996). *From our eyes: Learning from indigenous peoples*. Toronto: Garamond Press.

Quintasket, Christine [Mourning Dove]. (1981). *Cogewea, the half-blood: A depiction of the great Montana cattle range*. Lincoln: University of Nebraska Press.

Rosen, K. (Ed.). (1974). *The man to send rain clouds*. New York: Viking Press.

Silko, L. M. (1977). *Ceremony*. New York: Viking Press.

CHAPTER 4

Hinduism and Learning

Swathi Nath Thaker

Imagine, for a moment, that you are in a room surrounded by friends and family. There are people of all ages who have gathered to celebrate a festival. In order to commemorate the occasion, special decorations are displayed, particular rituals are performed, and specific food is prepared. Additionally, both children and adults perform dances and skits that illustrate the origins and details of the holiday. The elders share not only their memories of past festivities, but they also articulate the meaning and significance of the celebration through stories that have passed from generation to generation. This gathering is not only about celebrating, but also about personal growth.

When considering this example, it can be questioned whether the mentioned activities actually contain a learning component. There is no traditional classroom. There is no formal instructor. There is no written text. Instead, there is music, dance, and storytelling which serve as the "textbook" for this learning experience. Many of the Western perspectives on learning would argue that this does not represent true education. Instead, this form of knowledge would be compared to myths or folklore, which inevitably diminishes the value and validity of this type of information. However, is the ultimate goal of learning merely the attainment of factual data?

The Western notions of learning have, and still, dominate the field of adult education, with noncognitive forms of learning such as somatic learning and spirituality only recently emerging. While much of the Western literature on learning and knowing suggests that the mind and body are split, a number of cultures around the world do not believe in this dichotomy, and Hinduism is no exception. Hinduism, which is said to be over 4000 years old, defines itself according to the Vedas, the most ancient body of religious literature. While much of this content has long been unknown to most Hindus, it is still regarded as an absolute authority which reveals the fundamental truth. It is through these texts, which were originally shared vocally, that individuals come to appreciate multiple ways of learning and connecting to the world. Though Western belief teaches that an individual is empowered through himself or herself, Hinduism argues that true empowerment emerges through an understanding of the sources of knowledge, not just its components, which in turn leads to unity with the universe. Thus, life for Hindus becomes not merely about learning facts and figures, but also about developing wisdom by forming a connection between the mind, body, and spirit.

This chapter explores the philosophy of Hinduism and its views of learning and human development. First, a brief history and overview will be provided to ground the reader in the origins and basic characteristics of this ancient religion. Next, learning and development from a Hindu perspective will be examined. Finally, the chapter will conclude with a discussion of the modern Hindu. What does this philosophy look like in today's society? What are the implications of these changes?

WHAT IS HINDUISM?

Before one can begin to discuss the impact of Hinduism on the learning process and the construction of knowledge, it is important to have an understanding of the concept, on a historical as well as philosophical level. The term "Hindu" comes from a Persian word *hind*, or in Arabic *al-hind*, for the area of the Indus valley. This word is in turn derived from the Indo-Aryan *sindhu* meaning "ocean" or "river" and was utilized to originally distinguish between Muslims and non-Muslims (Flood, 2003). Later, toward the end of the 18th century, *Sindhu* was adopted by the British and its meaning was broadened to refer to individuals who were not Muslim, but also to indicate those who were not Sikh, Christian, or Jain. It was the British who also coined the term "Hinduism" (Hawley, 1991), and this origination has spurred debate about the validity of this label. However, millions of people in India and throughout the world continue to identify themselves as Hindu, and thus it can be argued that this term, whatever its origin, is significant for a large segment of the population.

The religion now known as Hinduism encompasses a vast range of practices and beliefs. It has no one founder and no centralized organization. Hindus throughout history have expressed multiple perspectives on the nature of divinity or ultimate reality. It is this richness and diversity that makes it difficult to pinpoint a comprehensive list of the religion's characteristics that would apply to all Hindus. However, it is this openness that forms the cornerstone of this philosophy. According to Hinduism, freedom of religious belief, worship and practice, and diversity of faiths are not incompatible with the unit of religion or religions. A significant consequence of this attitude in Hinduism is its spirit of tolerance. It is noted that individuals who praise their own religion and say that only their faith is true, do a disservice to their religion. Hinduism is not religion bound in its origins to a fixed point of time or to a personality. It is a variety of growing beliefs. Naturally enough, it became not only a way of life but also a view of life (Chennakesavan, 1974).

This notion of Hinduism representing a way of life has been echoed by a number of researchers (Boutte, 2002; Rinehart, 2004). There is no word in Indian languages that accurately corresponds to the English word *religion*, which entails assumptions that belief has primacy over practice, that a person can only belong to one religion, that tradition stems from textual, written revelation, and that religion is necessarily coherent (Flood, 2003). Instead, the word that is most commonly used, *dharma*, has a connotation that is far wider in scope. Hindu literature and traditions that examine this idea not only discuss God and God's purpose, but they also illustrate how society should be organized and even what one should and should not eat (Rinehart, 2004). Additionally, it is important to recognize that there has not always been a clear distinction among what are now known as religion, philosophy, and science. Therefore, when individuals began to explore these areas, the process was often "religious" in nature. For example, early mathematics partly developed in India to make accurate measurements in constructing locations to practice rituals.

This emphasis on the written word, which is found in a number of other theologies, needs to be discussed in relation to Hinduism. While it can be argued that South Asian cultures are highly textualized, this is in the widest sense of the term, as there are many oral traditions, some of which date back thousands of years. There are traditions of Vedic recitation in several regions of India that are said to function as 3000-year-old tape recordings (Witzel, 1997). This revelation of the Veda, verses believed to have been heard by the ancient sages as a symbol and legitimizing reference, is critical (Oberhammer, 1997, cited in Flood, 2003), and can be viewed as a defining feature of Hinduism. Thus, the concept of "text" needs to be reevaluated when utilized to discuss Hindu philosophy. Modern day texts typically have a clearly defined content as well as clearly identified authors. To most modern readers, the term "text" suggests a printed book, which we read silently. Yet much of what we now think of as Hindu texts were first preserved and transmitted as oral traditions meant to be recited and heard, not read from a written or printed page. Each recitation might include variations, elaborations, or explanations of earlier recitations, creating multiple versions of the same traditions with no one clearly identifiable composer or author. The variations in some instances may be the most informative parts of the text, because they may reflect the specific interests of a particular time period or region or group of people (Rinehart, 2004). This willingness not only to acknowledge, but also to accept such deviations again highlights the importance of honoring multiple perspectives and multiple truths.

This brief sketch of Hinduism illustrates the complexity of this term. From its historical underpinnings to its modern day meaning, the characteristics that comprise this concept remain unclear. However, whether one believes that Hinduism is specifically a religion or more broadly a philosophical view of life, what is clear is that millions of individuals across the world continue to utilize this framework not only to help them to grow and develop, but also to provide them with a life purpose. With this in mind, the next section will explore the developmental and learning process according to the philosophy of Hinduism.

LEARNING ACCORDING TO HINDUISM

Hinduism, whether viewed as a religion or as a way of life, offers its followers guidelines to becoming an enlightened individual. In Hindu theory there are two types of learning, each with its own goal and its own method. The first has the aim of gaining knowledge from the world, so it is outer directed. Its source is the environment, and its methodology is twofold—formal study of sacred writings and the informal interaction with the world known as experience. The second type of learning has self-understanding as its aim. Its source is the person's own spirit, and its methodology is introspection as achieved through meditation (Thomas, 1988).

When seeking to gain knowledge from the world, formal study of the scriptures under the direction of a wise *guru* (teacher) is essential. Such knowledge is neither instinctive nor available through inward reflection. And while personal experience in daily living and in observing one's society can furnish some of this information, much depends on formal study. For this, and other reasons, the connection between the teacher and student is critical and often one that is revered. This relationship will be explored in more detail later in this chapter.

When considering the second and more complex type of learning, namely self-understanding, several beliefs intersect to lead to this type of introspection. Central to this philosophy is the concept of justice. In their development, people get what they earn, what they deserve. Such a belief is contrary to a number of principles espoused by various Western sociologically oriented or environment-oriented theorists who argue that people are not solely responsible for their own development, but that their fate has been fashioned by environmental influences beyond their control. But in Hindu theory, the individual is clearly master of one's fate and captain of one's soul (Thomas, 1988). With this notion of development, the life of the body and the life of the soul must be considered separately. The body, according to Hinduism, is a passing illusion and is perishable. The essence of a human and the only lasting reality is the soul or mind, so one's psychic self becomes the object that determines the length of development.

Yet another approach to development of the Hindu male is known as the *twice-born man*. Both of the births implied in this term occur during a single lifetime on earth. The first birth takes place when the infant emerges from the mother's womb. The second occurs between late childhood and late adolescence at the time a child of an Aryan marriage is judged to be mature enough to begin studying the Vedas (Thomas, 1988). This point of initiation into the sacred knowledge of Hinduism signals the beginning of the spiritual development of a youth. The agent of this second birth is not the mother but, rather, the guru or teacher. For this reason, the young are taught never to offend their teacher, for it is the teacher who "causes the pupil to be born a second time by imparting to him sacred learning. It is often noted that this second birth is the best" (Renou, 1961, p. 109).

There are clear stages outlined for the Indian male during his life span that begins with the "second birth" on earth as he is initiated into the study of the Vedas. Beginning with the initiation, Hindu doctrine identifies four periods of life: (1) the student, (2) the householder or family man, (3) the hermit who escapes into a forest, and (4) the almsman who returns to society but abandons any attachment to worldly objects (Thomas, 1988).

The length of studentship is defined not in years but in mastery of the scriptures, vows, duties, rites, austerities, and techniques of meditation. The learner's daily life throughout this stage is filled with a host of prescribed rituals and study sessions with the guru. The revered guru-student relationship is one of high importance and can be found in a number of the ancient texts that outline the principles of Hinduism. For example, note the following narrative from the Mahabharat, an epic in itself, which contains a code of life, a philosophy of social and ethical relations which offers spiritual strength. The following tale, contained within this literature, highlights the sacred relationship of guru and student:

> Ekalavya witnesses the archery skill of Drona and wishes him to be his guru. However, Drona refuses, for a number of reasons, chief among them because he already has a pupil, Arjuna, to whom he has promised the title of greatest archer in the world. Disappointed, Ekalavya takes it upon himself to secretly watch Drona during his instruction. Through his absolute devotion to the art and ceaseless practice, Ekalavya's skills surpass those of Arjuna's. Arjuna's dream is shattered and Drona inquires how the youth has learned such an art. Though it can be argued that it was Ekalavya's devotion and determination that developed his success, he honors Drona by kneeling before him. Drona becomes upset when he realizes that Ekalavya has been watching him, as he has a loyalty to Arjuna. Thus, Drona asks Ekalavya for his right thumb as payment for this teaching, which he immediately offers out of gratitude, even though he knows he will no longer be able to practice archery.

This story illustrates the connection between student and master, on both sides. Drona felt a strong bond to his disciple, Arjuna, and helping him fulfill his dream of becoming the world's greatest archer. Thus, he asks Ekalavya for his thumb, knowing full well that this will make it impossible for the youth to be an archer. In turn, Ekalavya feels a deep reverence for Drona because he views him as his master and guide. It is through this respect that Ekalavya freely offers his thumb. While this tale does represent the notion of apprenticeship, as both Arjuna and Ekalavya were seeking to master a specific skill, it is important to realize that in Hindu philosophy, the guru-student relationship extends much further. Though Hinduism does allow for individuation, its purpose is spiritual growth, thus helping individuals to connect the mind and body.

The end of studentship is signified by a ceremony in which the male casts away his garb, shaves, pares his nails, washes his teeth, and has his hair cut. He then dons a new, more elaborate suit, including an umbrella, and other decorative items.

Once the male has completed his education, he is ready to begin the householder stage, which is initiated through marriage. Upon entering this phase, the householder assumes a heavy burden of responsibility, since he is expected to support the members of his family, It is this order that keeps the workaday world operating through householders assuming the roles of parents, administrators of government, producers of goods, traders, warriors, and educators (Thomas, 1988). In the third stage, the householder abandons all his belongings, takes with him the sacred fire and necessities for domestic sacrifices, and lives in the forest, either alone or with his wife. It is during this period of life that he observes the greatest austerities, exposing himself to fire and rain, sleeping on the bare ground, eating roots and fruit, and receiving money and/or goods hardly sufficient to sustain life. It is through these difficulties and the diligent study of sacred texts that the ascetic seeks to achieve complete union with the Supreme Soul, which is the ultimate goal. Although the hermit has given up his business affairs and mundane responsibilities, he has not separated himself entirely from society and remains available to advise others who would profit from his knowledge of the proper life. However, he does not long remain a recluse, for he soon abandons his forest dwelling to enter the final stage of development.

When he becomes a sannyasin, the devout Hindu forsakes all earthly ties and concern for his physical self, and he turns ever inward in final search of union with the Divine Reality. No longer is he obligated to observe the complex variety of rituals of the earlier stage, since the function of rituals has been to unite the believer with the Supreme Reality, and the sannyasin has now passed that brink. Since the crowning glory of Hinduism is the renunciation personified in the wandering merchant, all Hindus bow before a sannyasin and think it a privilege to serve him (Flood, 2003). The earthly end to this stage is death, with the soul proceeding beyond into the next life.

It is important to recognize that these phases are only applicable to Hindu males. Females did not, and still do not, undergo these same rites of passage to signify their development as women. Although today, girls in India attend schools along with boys, they were never meant to leave their family and take up studentship with a guru. This is because a woman's preparation for the householder stage takes place informally within the home, as the mother teaches her daughter about the responsibilities of being a wife and a mother. These skills are essential because it is only through marriage that a woman can continue her search for the ultimate purpose in life. It is only through her husband that she can also unite with the Supreme Reality. Although women have made many strides in India, this belief continues to illustrate the male-dominated view of Hinduism.

So, what do these stages tell us about the goal of development? Though only a small number of males will pass through all the phases mentioned above (Rinehart, 2004), and these phases are largely symbolic, they still offer both men and women an ultimate purpose, as both are seeking the same goal. Hinduism is sometimes called a religion of renunciation, rejection, or denial. The obligation of a Hindu is to renounce or reject the visible world with its illusory succession of lives and deaths in order to achieve relief from both the pains and the joys of mortality. So the key objective is not to attain happiness, pleasure, or success in a worldly sense but, rather, to win release from life. This goal of liberation is attained through a variety of ways, from mastering knowledge of the sacred writings to performing a multiplicity of rites. In order to distinguish between worldly happiness and the ultimate release from successive lives on earth, Hindu authors utilize the terms *kama* and *moksha*. While kama denotes the happiness enjoyed by ordinary mortals during their lifetime, moksha is the "supreme, unalloyed eternal happiness" enjoyed when the soul is ultimately merged again into the Eternal Mind or Soul (Iyer, 1969, p. 9).

The journey toward the ultimate goal of moksha is marked by transitional goals that are instrumental in attaining this final aim of development. These objectives are found in Hindu literature in two forms—as traits of the good person and as specific behaviors which reflect or comprise these qualities. The characteristics articulated in Hindu writings are clearly not unique to Hinduism and are found in other ethical systems as well. However, by emphasizing certain virtues over other possible ones, Hinduism lends its goals of development a recognizable spirit. The principal valued traits can be clustered into five groupings and are as follows: (1) studious and knowledgeable, particularly well versed in the religion's sacred literature; (2) disciplined, dutiful, devoted, loving, and obedient; (3) humble, self-effacing, unselfish, and self-sacrificing; (4) even-tempered, chaste, freed from desire and aversion, exempt from hate and inordinate affection, and pure of speech and thought; and (5) trusting in the correctness of Hindu doctrine (Thomas, 1988). When examined closely, it becomes evident that missing from the typical list of esteemed characteristics are such attributions as self-assertive, inquisitive, sensuous, enthusiastic, inventive, and independent of thought, all of which would be highly valued among Western society. Although heroes in Hindu epics often display a number of these traits, such features are generally not recognized as desirable in Hindu tradition.

In summary then, the desired direction for human development is depicted in Hinduism in three forms—as the general goal of liberation from the cycle of rebirths and deaths, as valued character traits, and as behaviors that serve as vehicles carrying the individual toward the ultimate goal of liberation.

HINDUISM IN THE 21st CENTURY

These ideas represent those of traditional Hindu theory. However, are these tenets still active in today's modern society? It can be argued that deviations from these traditional ways have occurred for a variety of reasons. An examination of present-day Indian society and of its history over the past two centuries suggests that the main force has been Western modernization, with a likely secondary force being people's daily observations of life around them.

A large body of evidence supports the argument that the

form of education which the British introduced into India in the mid-19th century became the most significant of the influences that have fostered the Western modernization of Indian society (Thomas, 1988). Western-style schooling was first brought to India by Christian missionaries. As private mission schools spread, they served as the initial channels for introducing Western values and knowledge into Indian society. Although during the ensuing decades traditional Hindu and Muslim schools continued to operate, each typically centering around a revered guru instructing youths in religious doctrine, such institutions greatly diminished in importance (Paranjoti, 1969). The dominant mode of formal education throughout the land became the British variety of secular schooling, with English as the chief language of instruction.

In this British form of schooling the great majority of India's intellectual and political elite of modern times learned Western science, logic, modes of inquiry, notions of social organizations, viewpoints toward individualism and human rights, concepts of human development, and more (Thomas, 1988). And while Western education was still limited to a minority of Indians during the colonial era, it did become increasingly widespread. Thus, when India achieved independence in 1947, political and educational leaders in the dominantly Hindu regions of the land had in their experience two major persuasions on which to draw, the Hindu and the Western, with minor traditions (such as Muslim and Buddhist) complicating the decision in certain districts. The leaders' problem was that of melding elements of Hinduism and the West into a harmonious blend that would serve as a foundation for modern nation-building. In addition, within education this effort to integrate the ancient and the modern was not entirely new. Since the late 19th century there have been attempts on a limited scale to combine Hindu tradition with Western science and social ideals so as to construct a curriculum that was spiritually Indian, yet suited to the demands of modern times.

The present-day task of developing government social policies and the schools' curriculum content have presented planners with difficult decisions, because so many Western notions about human development, scientific inquiry, and social organization conflict sharply with Hindu tradition. For example, two Hindu human development beliefs that clash with a Western egalitarian social philosophy have been those regarding caste and female inferiority (Thomas, 1988). Among modern-day Indians, Western schooling that includes concepts of widespread equal rights has somewhat eroded traditional Indian beliefs about caste and women's status, but clearly these Hindu traditions have not been eliminated. Even with an increasing number of Indian women now entering the workforce, the conceptualization of their role both in the home and in society has still not drastically changed. Furthermore, though over the past century or more females in Indian society have been accorded increasingly greater rights and status in comparison to males, that they are still considered to be inferior and thus should be submissive to males is attested by studies of the position of women in Indian society (Ray, 2000; Riessman, 2002; Sarkar, 2001).

It can be argued that Western beliefs, disseminated through channels of education, can account to a great degree for the digressions from Hindu theory found in today's Indian society. For example, though some individuals still seek to develop traditional Hindu social virtues, very few actually seek the ultimate life aim. Instead, an increasing number of individuals seek worldly ambitions such as obtaining a good education and/or a good job. These deviations are quite in keeping with the values and kinds of skills and knowledge fostered by a Western secular education, which is the variety of schooling officially advocated by the government.

As society continues to progress and technology advances, the Western perspective continues to dominate mainstream thought. Additionally, in order to remain competitive in today's global economy, countries are often forced to adopt the "American work ethic," and India is no exception. However, as noncognitive means of knowing have begun to be valued, elements from Eastern philosophies have begun to be adopted around the world. Yoga is one such practice. Yoga is an ancient spiritual practice that originated in India and is seen as a means to enlightenment. More specifically, these techniques provide a method for self-realization, allowing individuals to identify their own personal layers in order to understand their true identity. This process begins with physical pleasure, though this represents the smallest and most limited layer of the self. This self-indulgence of the senses, in Hinduism, is encouraged until one realizes that this type of pleasure seeking is incomplete in its meaning and gratification. Once this is recognized, it becomes possible to focus on gaining recognition from society or achieve worldly success, such as fame, wealth, and/or power. Although this level is broader in its sphere, it is still restricted because it is based on the concept that the well-being of the individual is separate from the well-being of others. Once one understands that promoting the little self is not rewarding, that person is ready to proceed to a more inclusive way of viewing the world. This requires a dedication to the well-being of society and an overall connection to humanity. Throughout this journey the ultimate goal is not only for self-actualization, but also to experience a union between one's self and the eternal. This process seeks to form a link between the body, mind, and spirit, and offers an alternate approach to knowing and relating to the world.

A number of yoga practices have been created to help people reach this union between the individual self and the Divine. For example, there is Bhakti yoga, which is designed for those who are grounded in emotions and feelings. In this form of yoga, God manifests in multiple forms so that the individual can develop a personal relationship with the Divine. The individual chooses a specific form of God for lifelong dedication. By focusing on developing a connection with one, the individual is opening up a gateway to the Supreme Reality. In contrast, Jnana yoga is suitable for those persons who are comfortable with ideas. This is a more intellectual path, where the individual seeks to develop an intuitive distinction between the little self and the Ultimate self. This is accomplished by learning, reflecting, and then "seeing" the limitations of the personal self, thus unifying with God. Raja yoga emphasizes meditation and other mental and physical exercises to help the individual overcome distractions, calm the mind, and concentrate on developing a connection with the Divine.

Many in the United States are familiar with Hatha yoga, which is associated with the postures and has gained popularity as yoga continues to grow and expand around the world. Due to this popularity, these postures are sometimes presented as entirely secular and nonspiritual in nature, but this would not be accurate when considering the origins of Hatha yoga. Traditionally, this form of yoga is a complete yogic path, including moral discipline, physical exercises such as postures and breath control, and meditation. It was created to provide a form of physical purification and training that would prepare individuals for Raja Yoga, which was described earlier. Though many in the West practice Hatha yoga solely for the health benefits rather than a path to enlightenment, it is important to realize that the ultimate goal of each of these forms of yoga is to lead to the knowledge of the true nature of reality. By suspending thought and no longer privileging the mind over the body, individuals are able to gain a deeper understanding of their relationship to others and to the universe as a whole.

Even though Indians are less focused on following the traditional way of life outlined earlier in this chapter, a number of its characteristics continue to influence the growth and development of Hindu individuals. For example, while the written word has become a popular vehicle for the transmission of knowledge, Hindus still rely on a number of other approaches when imparting information. I can still remember the stories that my grandmother used to share to help me better understand my heritage. She used these tales to not only teach me about the religious aspects of life, but also to illustrate the type of individual I should strive to be. It did not matter that the words were not in a written format—the absence of written text did not diminish the value or importance of the narratives. Instead, my grandmother was able to personalize the stories, conveying a message that impacts my life still today. While it can be argued that these variations alter the original meaning, it can also be noted that it is precisely these alterations that keep these stories alive by allowing the orator the opportunity to situate ancient words in current times.

The importance of storytelling is not only evident in the oral tradition of Hinduism. Dance, drama, and music are all utilized to convey the lessons that are contained in the ancient texts. For instance, through the art of classical Indian dance, individuals come to learn about the various Gods and Goddesses, their relationship to one another, and their significance. In a similar fashion, drama is used as a role-playing tool, allowing people the opportunity to act out scenarios and reflect on their magnitude. This is yet another way that knowledge is passed from one generation to the next, and it is this recounting, whether through stories, dance, or drama, that keeps Hinduism alive.

While this concept of narrative remains strong, it can still be questioned whether Hinduism is actually *practiced* in today's modern society. It cannot be denied that numerous changes have occurred over the centuries that this philosophy has been in existence. Adherence has weakened and rituals have been shortened to accommodate the fast pace of the 21st century. However, the core beliefs underpinning these customs remain strong and certain traditions even continue to be followed just as they were at the time of their inception. For example, though most individuals no longer live and study the Vedas with a guru, passage through the various stages of life is still extremely important and thus continues to be highlighted in practice. I can vividly recollect watching my brother undergo the ceremony to pass from studentship to the householder stage, where he actually did brush his teeth, get his haircut, carried a sunshade, and decided that he was indeed ready to enter marriage (as described earlier in this chapter). Even though this ritual is now more of a symbolic representation, the belief at the center of this practice remains unchanged. This rite of passage is still believed to help an individual reach the ultimate goal of liberation, and thus it, along with other similar customs, continue to be performed even in today's modern society.

SUMMARY

Throughout life, Hindus strive to become learned in multiple ways. It is not simply about developing cognitive skills, but rather to discover oneself as this is the only means and path to liberation and wisdom. However, this self-discovery is not the end of the spiritual journey, but rather a stepping stone to gaining a more holistic understanding of the universe. Though Western belief teaches that an individual is empowered through himself or herself, Hinduism argues that true empowerment emerges through an understanding of the sources of knowledge, not just its components, thus leading to unity with the universe which at times, requires a renouncing of the self and worldly possessions. This is particularly poignant during the last stage of life, where individuals abandon their home and belongings and set forth on a pilgrimage or seek sanctuary in an ashram, which is a spiritual hostel. This type of journey still takes place today, as it is believed that this passage leads to true enlightenment through unification of the mind and body. Thus, life for Hindus becomes not about the acquisition of knowledge, but about developing wisdom through gaining an understanding of oneself through a holistic manner.

This notion of foregoing identity in order to reach a state of higher understanding is powerful, and often neglected in Western thought. There is a strong emphasis on individuation in the West which is not readily apparent in Hinduism. The Hindu learner continually strives to understand the larger picture and his or her connection to the universe as a whole. It can be argued that this mentality allows the learner to be open to varying sources of knowledge. By honoring a variety of forms of knowledge, such as through meditation and stories, and not relying solely on the printed word, the Hindu learner is able to obtain a level of spiritual being that is often difficult for the Western student. As the Western educational system begins to value other ways of knowing, its learners will have an opportunity to focus less on the self and increasingly on forming a unity with the world at large.

REFERENCES

Boutte, V. (2002). *The phenomenology of compassion in the teachings of Jiddu Krishnamurti (1895–1986)*. Lewiston, NY: The Edwin Mellen Press.

Chennakesavan, S. (1974). *A critical study of Hinduism*. New York: Asia Publishing House.

Flood, G. (Ed.). (2003). *The Blackwell companion to Hinduism*. Malden, MA: Blackwell Publishing.

Hawley, J. S. (1991). Naming Hinduism. *Wilson Quarterly, 63,* 20–34.

Iyer, K. B. (1969). *Hindu ideals*. Bombay: Bharatiya Vidya Bhavan.

Paranjoti, V. (1969). *East and west in Indian education*. Lucknow: Lucknow Publishing House.

Ray, S. (2000). En-gendering India: Woman and nation in colonial and postcolonial narratives. Raleigh, NC: Duke University Press.

Renou, L. (1961). *Hinduism*. New York: Braziller.

Riessman, C. K. (2002). Analysis of personal narratives. In J. Gubrium & J. A. Holstien (Eds.), *Handbook of qualitative research*, 2nd ed. (pp. 923–958.). Thousand Oaks, CA: Sage.

Rinehart, R. (Ed.). (2004). *Contemporary Hinduism: Ritual, culture, and practice*. Santa Barbara, CA: ABC-CLIO.

Sarkar, T. (2001). *Hindu wife, Hindu nation : Community, religion and cultural nationalism*. New Delhi: Permanent Black.

Thomas, R. M. (Ed.). (1988). *Oriental theories of human development: Scriptural and popular beliefs from Hinduism, Buddhism, Confucianism, Shinto, and Islam*. New York: Peter Lang Publishing.

Witzel, M. (1997). *Inside the texts, beyond the texts: New approaches to the study of the Vedas*. Cambridge, MA: Harvard University Press.

CHAPTER 5

Māori Concepts of Learning and Knowledge

Brian Findsen and Lavinia Tamarua

He aha te mea nui o te ao?
He tangata, he tangata, he tangata.
(What is the most important thing in the world? It's
people, it's people, it's people.)

The above proverb from Māori traditions stresses the centrality of people to any activity of living. Learning is no exception. Traditional Māori learning has always been lifelong and lifewide, long before these concepts became fashionable in adult education circles and beyond. The term *mātauranga Māori* has been used in a variety of contexts to indicate a "body of knowledge" as well as to indicate a "type of knowledge." There has been considerable confusion and misunderstanding over the meaning of the term. A common practice has been to discuss mātauranga Māori as a body of Māori knowledge that is generally held within the Māori world (Royal, 2004, p.14). Embedded within the traditions of mātauranga Māori can be recognised Māori cultural practices of teaching and learning processes. Similarly, *ako*, the Māori word for learning, necessarily entails a historical and cultural dimension and is also the word for teaching (see further discussion later in this chapter). Before Freire (1972) explained the concepts of teacher-student and student-teacher, the term *ako* did not differentiate between those who dispense knowledge and those who acquire it. Knowledge, in Māori traditions, is always a collective entity so that any knowledge acquired by individuals also belongs to the tribe.

INTRODUCTION

In this chapter we introduce and discuss some Māori concepts of learning and knowledge in a variety of ways: in the context of our own relationships and identification with *Māoritanga* (things Māori); from traditional Māori formulations of learning and knowledge; the historical and political dynamics of *Māori tino rangatiratanga* (self-determination) in *Aotearoa* New Zealand. Necessarily, too, we place Māori knowledge and dissemination in the context of the Treaty of Waitangi signed in 1840, given its primacy of place in contemporary Aotearoa New Zealand legislature and governmental attempts to make the country truly bicultural. Aotearoa is in fact the Māori name for New Zealand. Its use as in Aotearoa New Zealand illustrates the parity of esteem of the Māori and European names for the country. Education by Māori for Māori is inextricably connected to initiatives in preserving their language and culture in a continuing quest for Māori sovereignty. In acknowledging the importance of historical context, we also locate traditional knowledge in the indigenous social structure. Finally, we consider the character of Māori learning in contemporary Aotearoa New Zealand but necessarily linked in a political context where Māori educators have sought to emphasise Māori-controlled knowledge and learning.

In this situation we need to state our positionality in relation to the construction of Māori knowledge. As first author, a New Zealander, an adult educator, and student of Māoritanga, I offer an "insider" perspective, having completed a Certificate in Māori Studies in 1983 at the University of Waikato; as a *Pakeha* (European), I offer an "outsider" viewpoint, unavoidably Eurocentric to a degree. I can never be bicultural in the same way as a Māori person who is immersed in the dominant culture and subject to its oppressive power relations; I choose as a member of the dominant colonising group to better understand Māori concepts and perspectives. The issue of the exploitative nature of much research concerning Māori undertaken by Pakeha (Jahnke & Taiapa, 1999) is to the forefront of my mind but I am also comforted by assertions that non-Māori academics and researchers have their place, as long as they demonstrate sufficient skill, knowledge, and sensitivity to Māori norms in the process (see Stokes, 1985, cited in Jahnke & Taiapa, 1999).

As the second author, my positionality and cultural knowledge that is expressed in this chapter is in the context of my tribal and *whakapapa* (ancestral) connections and also the formal education experienced living in an urban society. I was born in Auckland, Aotearoa New Zealand. My father is Cook Island-Māori, born in his family village of Matavera, situated in the North-West region on the mainland Island of Rarotonga, in the Pacific region. My mother is of *Ngati Whatua* and *Ngā Puhi* tribal affiliation, and Pakeha ancestry as well. Our tribal territory stretches from *Tamaki Makaurau* (Auckland) to the North-West surrounding *Kaipara* region then further north on the Northland Peninsula, in Aotearoa New Zealand. As an "insider" of "being and acting" Māori, my cultural understandings have been influenced through the combination of my *whakapapa* (ancestral links) and my formal educational background. The socialisation and cultural practices inherent and valued by my parents were situated through teaching and learning experiences of exposure and demonstration (Pere, 1982). It is not my intention as the second author to generalise or attempt to make statements about Māoridom but instead to provide an insight into some of the contemporary and traditional cultural understandings familiar to me. Therefore, as a Māori researcher, sharing common cultural experiences and more importantly reporting on one's own culture has its advantages but can also be a setting for tensions. The obvious advantage is that the researcher has insight into ways of "doing" and in many cases of "being" that distinguish how a person approaches, plans, and makes contact with the people who will be researched. Within this framework, researching Māori and being a Māori researcher involve a deeper critical understanding of how one positions oneself as a researcher and also as one of those being researched (Mead, 2003). Hence, this chapter represents an interweaving of two complementary perspectives of Māori knowledge and learning through our respective subjective lens but one that tries to avoid a unitary perspective, given the complexities of Māori lives immersed in tribal identity (Doherty, 2005).

HISTORICAL CONTEXT

It is believed that Māori *iwi* (tribes) travelled from Hawaiki many centuries ago, as described in myths and legends. It is fundamental to understand that the term *Māori* is a generic one used primarily by non-Māori to describe collective tribes, as if one entity. The iwi is the basic unit of affiliation. Doherty explains the complexity of the concept of mātauranga Māori (Māori knowledge) in relation to tribal identity:

> There is a danger in Mātauranga Māori, if the reader or researcher has a limited understanding of Māori, it can be viewed as another form of colonisation, in that Mātauranga Māori attempts to homogenise Mātauranga that is held by Māori; it ignores the fact that Māori are an eclectic tribal people. While there are similarities in the language and exoteric versions of history, each tribe has its own histories, stories, and explanations unique to them. (2005, p. 2)

The above quote reinforces the importance of tribal identity based on the original migration of tribes to different geographical regions of Aotearoa. Obviously, this pattern of settlement of tribes was heavily disturbed by successive waves of European migrants, including missionaries, whalers, sealers, timber traders, and farmers. The New Zealand wars (erroneously dubbed "Māori wars" by many Pakeha) of the mid-19th century between Pakeha and Māori (and occasionally between tribes) principally related to contestation over resources, mainly land. To tribes, the *whenua* (land) (in essence, *Papatuanuku*, the Earth Mother) has special spiritual significance and is a collective *taonga* (special gift) to be treasured. The under-estimation by Pakeha of Māori spiritual attachment to the land has been historically one of the major sources of conflict.

Over the course of European occupation of New Zealand, there have been several ideological bases for interaction with indigenous Māori. Initially, it was one of conversion to a European worldview inclusive of Christianity via the work of missionaries; later ideological forces included assimilation, integration, and biculturalism. Under assimilation policies, European agencies (schools) were expected to bring Māori children into the ways of Pakeha culture, using such means as active discouragement of the use of Māori language on school grounds. Its eventual outcome would have been the eventual demise of Māori culture altogether. Integration, on the other hand, worked on the premise that there should be a combination of the best features of both contributing cultures. The reality in school contexts was the expectation of Māori children becoming like Pakeha while the dominant group had few pressures to reciprocate. More recently, other ideologies of multiculturalism (acknowledging the growing ethnic pluralism within New Zealand society) and biculturalism (setting up the legal framework for Māori and Pakeha to share resources, in special recognition of Māori as *tangata-whenua*, first people of the land) have assumed importance. These patterns of domination are not dissimilar to some other countries' experiences (see Mason, 1971, for an elaborated discussion on this theme), but essentially they comprise negotiation of power relations between dominant (Pakeha) and subordinate (Māori) groups. In contemporary Aotearoa New Zealand, these forms of ideological domination continue to exist side by side but the official view is that New Zealand is a bicultural country where Māori is the official language (while English is the most widely spoken) and in practice Government provides protection of Māori treasures, including Education, in accord with the principles derived from the Treaty of Waitangi (discussed further below).

TRADITIONAL KNOWLEDGE AND LEARNING

Māori society, or more accurately each tribe within Māori-tanga, derives its identity from the original *waka* (ancestral canoe) and its eventual settlement location in Aotearoa New Zealand. Each *iwi* has *hapū* (sub-tribes) made of *whānau* (extended families). Historically, the whānau formed the essential functional tasks for individuals and still does today though members are likely to be distributed across many locations, especially in the larger cities. As described by Hoskins: " 'Whānau' as a collective extended family network was the basic social and economic unit of Māori society and operated with the hapû to sustain community life at all levels" (2005, p. 2). Hence, the social structure of traditional Māori society begins with the ancestral canoe from which emerges tribal identity; the subtribe and extended families become the operational units for learning throughout a tribe.

Traditional learning entailed both formal and informal contexts. In the formal environment, the *marae* (communal meeting place, including the *whare whakairo* or carved meeting house and the *wharekai* or dining room) dominated the tribe's daily world. On the marae there were *hui* (literally, meetings, but inclusive of all kinds of activities, including learning events) at which tribal members discussed issues and consolidated their collective knowledge. According to Durie (2001, p. 72), a marae is indeed a forum where "what is important . . . is not necessarily the physical structure, but the exercise of encounters and values that might otherwise remain dormant or seem at odds with the wider community." The marae was, and indeed still is, a centre for tribal and Māori community activities crucial to the maintenance of tribal identity.

Marae encounters, prior to European contact, included a central space to welcome visitors (*manuhiri*), to negotiate the business of civil life, to clarify what constituted appropriate behaviour (e.g., for women or men), and to learn tribal genealogy or more generally, how one relates to prior occupants of this place. An example of the importance of the marae relates to how visitors are welcomed into the tribe by the hosts. Usually a male preserve, the hosts and visitors engaged in speech-making wherein the participants often displayed considerable oratory, sharing stories of the past and present but importantly functioning to find points of mutual interest, especially in terms of genealogy (shared ancestors). This responsibility fell to male elders as the public face of the tribe, the women occupying more private spaces such as in the dining room and kitchens (but considered no less important in terms of the extent of the welcome). Hence, young boys and girls were acculturated into the important norms and routines (*tikanga*) of that tribe and were socialised from a very early age into suitable behaviours. So, in the traditional tribal setting, learning was formally structured, based on a hierarchy but also gender-based. Boys learned skills such as how to engage in oratory and extensive memorisation related to genealogy; girls learned supportive roles such as hospitality, weaving, and caring.

It is important to acknowledge the numerous concepts in operation beneath the surface in Māori society, emanating from *Te Ao Māori Tawhito* (the ancient Māori world). Myths and legends of Māori abound, related back to the creation myth where *Ranginui* (the Sky Father) and *Papatuanuku* (Earth mother) created the gods (their children). These gods took charge of specific living domains: the forests; the elements; war; the sea; cultivated plants and uncultivated plants (e.g., the fernroot). One of the gods, *Tane Mahuta*, was responsible for the creation of humans, moulding the female body out of *onetapu*, the sacred earth of Papatuanuku, and breathing life into her.

It may not be easy to connect Māori mythology with modern learning but there is a definite strong link. Creation entailed the integration of land, sea, and the sky, all having spiritual significance. The traditional practice of caring for the natural environment relates to the cooperation of *Tāne* (god of the forests), *Tangaroa* (god of the sea), and other superior beings. Māori showed respect for their environment by conducting rituals for the gods and enacting prayers or incantations prior to consuming the products of the natural environment (fish, birds, trees for housing, etc.). Today, in modern New Zealand society, many public meetings, including both Māori and Pakeha, begin with a prayer, a mark of respect to the ancestors and to those people present. This is most evident when food is to be consumed.

In Māori myths there are numerous stories of characters who have achieved considerable feats. Prominent among these heroes is *Maui* who snared the sun so that we have warmth today; but he is most noted for his cheeky ventures where he displayed outstanding leadership. The tales provided early Māori with models of behaviour where important virtues were displayed. Hence, story-telling has been a prominent mode of learning for the community wherein good memory and an eye for detail were acclaimed in primarily an oral tradition.

In the traditional Māori world certain spiritual concepts relevant to all spheres of living (e.g., education, justice, health) were emphasised and permeated all learning contexts. According to Mead (2003), the source of *tapu* (sacred life force; wellness) is inherited through closeness to chiefly lines but every person has personal *tapu*. It is a fluid concept but relates to one's integrity, respect, and connectedness to community. It is important to preserve one's sacred state; hence, there are "rules" of expected behaviours related to personal space, the body, and death. For instance, one observes the rules of tapu at a *tangihanga* (funeral ceremony) by washing hands or sprinkling water over oneself after shaking hands with everyone or after leaving the cemetery. Other instances are not passing food over one's head and not stepping over the feet of persons lying down in the meeting house. Extensions of tapu continue today and these norms are learned both through formal occasions and informal mixing of family members.

In some instances, where knowledge was perceived as specialised and sacred, it was passed on to specific individuals of higher status (usually seniors in the tribe) for protection on behalf of the whole tribe. As commented by Jahnke and Taiapa, "the institution of tapu underpinned all rituals and learning processes as a vehicle for the protection and respect of associated knowledge" (1999, p. 43). In contrast, practices of everyday life (such as eating) were considered *noa* (profane, ordinary) and did not require prayers to precede their use.

The concept of *mana* (social status; prestige) is also important in both the traditional world and contemporary life. While
some mana may be inherited it is through one's achievements
that it can be enhanced or diminished. Famous Māori rugby
players such as Waka Nathan are accorded high mana; most
teachers would expect to have mana in their respective communities. Hence, personal development through education can enhance mana; learning is one avenue for its enhancement.

A third important concept is the *mauri* (life principle) of
people. The expression of *"Tihei mauri ora"* which often pre-
cedes a male about to conduct a formal speech might be para-
phrased as "Here I am, and I have something worth saying."
The mauri acts as an active sign of life and if somebody appears
unwell, it is likely there is something wrong with that person's
mauri. Hence, it is in everyone's interests to preserve the life
force of a person, one of the functions of a good teacher.

In traditional society learning was certainly viewed as lifelong and its intergenerational aspects have always been emphasised. As mentioned before, the central place for the collective
learning of the tribe has been the marae (carved meeting house
and courtyard). It is here that hosts assemble for important ceremonial occasions including to welcome *manuhiri* (visitors) to
the centre of community life. In this context, traditional learning was certainly gender and seniority based. A case in point is
that of the art of *whakairo* (carving), seen as a man's task; weaving seen as a woman's. Within the tribal structure, the status
of elders was high, in acknowledgement of their lifelong experiences providing them with a knowledge base to be shared
with younger members. On ceremonial occasions the men tend
to take precedence in the public sphere, as in conducting the
whaikōrero (speech-making), while women operate more in the
private sphere, as in preparing dining rooms for guests.

It is important to note that ancestral knowledge was holistic, relating to the entire repertoire of human capabilities. In
Māori mythology, Tāne Mahuta (god of the forest) handed
down three baskets of knowledge to the tribes of Aotearoa to
be cared for and used in appropriate contexts: *Kete tūāuri*: peace,
goodness, and love; *Kete tūātea*: prayers, incantations, and ritual;

Kete aronui: war, agriculture, woodwork, and stonework. In the workplace of the Auckland University of Technology, inside the meeting house there is a carving where these three baskets are profiled, providing the message to students to be aware of the diverse forms of knowledge open to them in this institution.

Everything in the Māori world was alive, all living things were related, and there was no distinction or separation between nature and culture that is found in Western thinking/ understandings. The earliest ancestors and their immediate descendants determined traditional behaviours characteristic of natural phenomena, men and women, and other life forms. Sometimes these phenomena were used to satisfy human needs as seen from the mythical trickster hero, Maui, who acquired fire from the sun and pulled up a fish from the sea that became *Aotea*, the North Island of Aotearoa New Zealand (Orbell, 1995).

As will be discussed further in the contemporary scene, most of these historical patterns persist, especially in the rural environment where tribal identity is still quite tangible. Younger Māori, especially those in urban contexts where traditions have been severed from the traditional base, are not always cognisant of their ancestral links and may struggle to identify themselves as belonging to a tribe. However, some pan-tribal marae based in cities, such as Hoani Waititi in West Auckland, are doing sterling work to reinvigorate Māoritangi, sometimes in conjunction with local schools.

GUIDING PRINCIPLES FOR
TEACHING AND LEARNING

While the above overarching concepts of tapu, mana, and mauri are intertwined in any learning situation and are linked closely to personal attributes, there are other principles that are commonly invoked in educational circles to explain the priorities for Māori learning.

Hemara (2000) has written about Māori pedagogies particularly exploring traditional teaching, learning, and childrearing patterns. He has focussed on the early childhood curriculum, *Te Whāriki*, which has been published by New Zealand's Ministry of Education, in which four fundamental principles are discussed:

1. *Whakamana*—the empowerment of *mokopuna* (grandchildren) to learn and grow;

2. *Kotahitanga*—the holistic aspect of learning;

3. *Whānau tangata*—consideration of the wider world of which a child is a part (including *whānau*);

4. *Ngā Hononga*—the responsive and reciprocal relationships with people, places, and things.

Arising from these principles are five strands of well-being, belonging, contribution, communication, and exploration.

The important point about this conceptualization of learning based on principles is that it is not exclusive to young children but encapsulates the whole of life. These principles and strands permeate all learning and provide a basis for curriculum (in its widest sense) in all spheres of education.

Taking just one of these concepts, *kotahitanga*, literally, to be as one, provides the imperative to bring people together. In historic times, the tribe and families were sustained through kotahitanga i.e., close-knit families sharing a common understanding of history, validated through the reciting of ancestral connections, songs, and proverbs, such as the one which begins this chapter. Hence, kotahitanga can engender cooperation or support in a learning context. In a learning situation, kotahitanga emphasises a unification of purpose and the opportunity to explore options to enhance beneficial relationships. The essence of kotahitanga is embodied in this proverb: *Ki nga whakaeke haumi* meaning "Ally yourself with those who have already banded together."

All learning typically links with four primary dimensions: *taha wairua* (the spiritual side), *taha hinengaro* (thoughts and feelings), *taha tinana* (the physical side), and *taha whatumanawa* (emotional). These primary dimensions encapsulated a Māori theoretical framework of development that depicted a series of transformations. These transformations could best be explained from the traditional knowledge of *Te Kore*, when the earth was void, followed by *Te Pō* (the world of darkness), *Te Ao Mārama* (the world of light), and *Tihe Mauriora* (the beginning of a human's life on earth) (Macfarlane, 2004). These traditional phenomena described the "beginning-of-the-end" of the human lifespan. Macfarlane (2004, p. 40) explained that "when a person dies, the spirit travels to *Te Rēinga*, the northernmost part of *Te Ika-a-Māui* (the North Island in Aotearoa New Zealand), the place of departure for the mythical homeland of Hawaiki." This then is the end of what may be recognised as the human lifespan, but not the end of one's being.

Irwin (1984) incorporated three of these dimensions to describe a Māori holistic worldview of development where body, mind, and spirit are not separate entities but interlinked depicting the concept of "wholeness" as well as being able to explain when an individual experiences a sense of "loss of wholeness." Durie's (2001) *Whare Tapa Whā* model, employed in health education environments, extends Irwin's model by adding and acknowledging the concept of family as a significant connection to one's ancestry. Durie's model is based on the four walls of a house, each side complementing each other representing "completeness" of a person.

As described by Doherty (2005, p. 3), learning was and still is integrated into larger frameworks of meaning, wherein "the transmission of knowledge of all kinds involved the integration of both metaphysical and technical considerations." For instance, the cultivation of the sweet potato required both a knowledge of cultural practices as well as technical skill in planting, harvesting, and storing. Learning in this less formal way relies on cultural dynamics including orthodox transmission of knowledge, strategic mentoring, and peer activities.

Traditional Euro-western theories have tended to view human development from a compartmentalised, disciplined approach beginning at the prenatal stage and ending in later adulthood. The above approaches stress different elements of humanity: holism, lifelong continuity, and the metaphysical.

The Māori word *ako* literally means "to teach and to learn" (Bishop & Glynn, 2000). There is no defining of each word as a separate concept, which is very different from the Western interpretation of both words teaching and learning (Metge, 1984). A similar concept, *ākonga Māori* has been used to also mean Māori learners and refer to a preferred Māori way of teaching and learning, which relates to traditional as well as present modes of everyday Māori learning (Smith, 1987). These concepts, along with others that are used to describe Māori teaching/learning practices, are not homogeneous to all Māori, but are traditional concepts that are practical and can be applied in multiple and varied ways.

Traditionally, Māori teaching/learning went hand in hand and integrated both theory and practice in formal and informal learning settings. Learning can be understood as a gradual process that emerges from practical learning experiences to maturity (Hemara, 2000). This learning process reflects similar socially constructed learning theories of development of children being scaffolded within their zone of proximal development (Vygotsky, 1978). However, in Māori tradition every person is recognized as a learner throughout the process. Some people are recognized to be more learned through their experiences and responsibilities so that the "balance of *mana* (prestige) is maintained and encouraged" through a process that is reciprocal between both learner and teacher (Pere, 1994, p. 54).

THE WIDER SOCIO-HISTORICAL CONTEXT

At the time of the signing of the Treaty of Waitangi in 1840 between a numerical majority of Māori and a growing minority of new European settlers, the intention was to provide a blueprint for subsequent relationships between indigenous Māori and citizens of the British Crown. In the words of prominent Māori educator, Ranginui Walker (1980, p. 103):

The Treaty proclaimed the Queen's sovereignty over New Zealand, and guaranteed the Māori people exclusive and undisturbed possession of their lands, forests and fisheries. But the Crown was to have the sole right to purchase land. In return, Māori were to be given full rights and protection as British citizens.

While the original intent is indicated in Walker's words, the actual implementation has resulted in ongoing struggle between Māori and Pakeha. As pointed out by Jones et al. (1995, p. 172), "for many Māori every aspect of social, political and economic life is connected to the Treaty of Waitangi." While to many Pakeha the Treaty is mere history, for most Māori it is a vital document in determining their daily lives. In recent times, the Government has moved away from an emphasis on textual interpretation to establishing a set of principles for social policy, including educational decision-making.

The Treaty of Waitangi provides much of the policy context for Māori self-determination and what counts as knowledge in officially bicultural Aotearoa New Zealand today. Importantly, three principles derived from the Treaty are prominent in current Government social policy—protection of cherished possessions such as language; partnership (moving forward on an equal power basis); participation (the rights of Māori to active citizenry, including equality of educational opportunity and outcomes). It is quite common to observe these principles hard-wired into the charters of educational institutions as a means to try to ensure that Pakeha adhere to them in practice.

A contemporary illustration of the struggle of Māori and contestation with Pakeha for education resources is in the reconstruction of the former Adult Learning and Reading Assistance Federation (ARLA), established in 1982, into the bicultural organisation of Literacy *Aotearoa*. The Federation's aim was to develop accessible quality literacy provision for the people of Aotearoa. A significant step, as described by indigenous literacy educator, Bronwyn Yates (1996, p. 106), was carried out in 1989 when the Federation decided to "move towards sharing the government grants to the national organisations equally between the Māori and *tauiwi* (non-Māori) literacy development and co-ordination." In effect, this decision, in accord with prin-

ciples emanating from the Treaty, set the platform for the enhanced provision of Māori literacy but importantly under the
control of Māori leadership.

A CONTEMPORARY PERSPECTIVE

In discussing Māori concepts, traditional tribal structures
need to be analyzed to provide the basis for the social construction of knowledge. While tribes were originally concentrated in
particular geographical areas, the reality now, after massive ur-
banisation, is that Māori people are scattered throughout the
country though usually anchored to their tribal identity. Knowledge is a treasure, unevenly distributed (on the basis of authority
and prestige), though highly valued; some of it is sacred and
controlled traditionally by *tohunga* (experts). While there is
much in common among tribes (based on traditional practices),
there are also significant differences, related to marae protocol.
Much knowledge is constructed and reinforced via meetings
held on marae where local customs are emphasised and extended family socialisation occurs. However, especially in urban
settings, some of the traditional aspects of learning have been
diminished and new social practices established.

It is necessary to reflect on the reality that the interests of
many Māori are different from those of most Pakeha. The relative emphasis placed on different forms of knowledge should be
linked to this reality. The primary tension underlying the contested terrain of education between Māori and Pakeha, as exemplified in the example of the early times for Literacy Aotearoa,
is summarised by Jones et al. (1995, p. 195) in Figure 5.1. While
arguably this is a simplistic portrayal of the different major orientations of the respective dominant and subordinate groups—
given that there is considerable variation within the groups—it
does provide a snapshot of different orientations and valuing of
what counts as knowledge (Young, 1971).

One of the prominent features of New Zealand life is
the increasing autonomy claimed by Māori in accord with self-
determination. This bid by Māori for greater control over their

Pakeha Interests	Māori Interests
Pakeha culture, language, knowledge	Māori culture, language, knowledge
Acculturation, assimilation	Validity and legitimacy of Māori
"We are one people."	"We are Māori."
Domination	Survival
Maintain status quo	Work for change

Figure 5.1 Educational interests of Māori and Pakeha

lives is mirrored in other parts of the world where indigenous peoples are making serious efforts to reclaim political, economic, and educational sovereignty. As Māori have been disenfranchised from much of government-funded education (as in evidence through historical national statistics of underachievement), their solution has been to rebuild Māori collective consciousness through establishing their own sites of learning where control is in their own hands. Knowledge is defined and constructed by Māori for Māori and learned in culturally appropriate ways.

In line with increasing Māori sovereignty, Māori have sought to establish their own alternatives to European-dominated knowledge and modes of learning. Importantly, as identified by Stewart-Harawira (1997, p. 328):

> At the heart of Māori intervention initiatives are educational programmes which are underpinned by the notion of whānau. In these programmes, the notion of whānau is being reconstituted as the fundamental means for the reclaiming of both identity and autonomy (tino rangatiratanga).

WHĀNAUNGATANGA: BEING FAMILY

There are strong links between Māori teaching/learning practices and the significance of group-oriented learning and reciprocity. Teaching/learning experiences demonstrate learning taking place within the nuclear and extended family where everyone who participates learns something new (Hemara, 2000). Both learning and teaching are based on methods of preferred Māori pedagogies that are embedded within the practices of whānaungatanga (Metge, 1984).

The composition of the Māori whānau (extended family) has a collectivist or societal orientation rather than containing solely or primarily individualistic properties (Pere, 1982). Makereti Papakura (1986) described the traditional social organization of Māori culture centred around the people rather than the self. She explained that Māori individuals thought only of their people, and were absorbed in their family, just as the family was absorbed in the subtribe and the subtribe in the tribe. Individual learning is not excluded from the composition of whānau but is an essential characteristic of teaching/learning embedded in the everyday events that occur within the family members, which is encouraged (Hohepa, McNaughton & Jenkins, 1996).

Interpersonal skills play a vital role in the development of family socialization practices. The responsibilities of each family member incorporate the view that teaching/learning is very much dependent on each member of the family to nurture and support one another in a reciprocal manner. The inclusiveness of other family members is recognized through the process of reciprocity and exchange of knowledge and responsibilities that is shared by the group. Traditionally Māori children are taught from a very young age that their existence within the family and community relies on their ability to coexist with others. The *tuakana-teina* (older-younger) relationship expresses this type of learning especially between older and younger siblings. For example, a fundamental principle under which the practice called *te kōhanga reo* (Māori language nest) operates and organizes activities is that children learn about family responsibilities of sharing, caring, and working together (Hohepa, McNaughton & Jenkins, 1996).

It is significant that the definition of whānau is not rigid. While in English the idea of extended family is close to this concept, it is often used figuratively in day-to-day life. For instance, when adult educators gather in a Māori context, after appropriate protocols of welcome, the assembly may be addressed as "whānau" to suggest a commonality of purpose, a collective enterprise where it is important to care for others' well-being. This point is epitomised by the usually generous hospitality of iwi/whānau to visitors and the balance between achieving tasks and fostering relationships at a social gathering.

Over the past two decades or so there have been major strategic education initiatives developed by Māori themselves as part of their cultural and linguistic renaissance. This has been a combined result of inspired leadership from the top (for example, through the efforts of leaders such as Pita Sharples in West Auckland) and grassroots mobilisation. The first such scheme was that of the establishment of *te kōhanga reo* (Māori language nests) where the focus is upon oral Māori language, immersing children in a total Māori immersion context. The learning emphasised in these preschool environments reflects a whānau focus, entailing a holistic approach of experiential learning. The rapid development of language nests from the first in Pukeatua in 1981 has been startling. From around 50 in 1982 the movement had mushroomed to over 800 in 1993 and is still strong today. Their success in developing fluent speakers of Māori demanded an urgent response from the state to produce teachers in the mainstream system with capabilities of teaching these children. In higher education colleges, "fast track" Māori-oriented training programmes were set up to meet this demand. Overall, the te kōhanga reo movement proved successful across several domains: ensuring the survival of Māori language; enhancing Māori organisational capacity through mobilisation of whānau; providing a viable alternative to mainstream Pakeha-controlled learning environments; eventually, after initial reluctance from the state, to secure a firmer funding base for Māori knowledge (Jones et al., 1995).

The logical outcome of the success of te kōhanga reo was to arrange for similar culturally relevant learning opportunities for children further up the education system. The *kura kaupapa Māori* movement triggered alternative Māori-controlled learning sites in the equivalent of primary education and subsequently secondary education. While the pedagogy of kura kaupapa Māori schools is linked to Māori-preferred teaching and learning methods the curriculum necessarily conforms to national guidelines. Hence, a major outcome is that such children become bilingual and bicultural, reinforcing their iwi/Māori identity. At a political level, the kura kaupapa Māori schooling-type was legitimated by inclusion within the Education Amendment Act of 1989.

Not surprisingly, the next step was the setting up of *whare wānanga* (higher education institutions) to provide learning opportunities for adults, primarily Māori. In an article which explains the tensions and contradictions inherent in establishing these institutions with respect to the state, McCarthy (1996) stresses that these contemporary forms of higher education share the features of responding to low participation rates of Māori in higher education; an ideological base which is distinctly iwi/Māori based; they constitute part of a wider pan-tribal plan to consolidate self-determination. The fundamental issue for these institutions has been whether to take public funding from the Government (as made possible in the 1990 Act) and conform to the strictures of surveillance (for instance, in terms of quality assurance mechanisms) or to be independent (thus dependent on scant resources of a poorer financial base yet more fully autonomous). So far, the preference has been for the former option to ensure survival yet to endeavour to construct such institutions according to Māori values.

Outside the formal system of education in the field of adult and community learning, there have been several Māori-propelled initiatives. Te kōhanga reo is both a preschool movement and an adult education movement—Māori parents are organically involved in its development and recognise the need for themselves to learn the Māori language or build upon rudimentary knowledge. One of the classic successes of the renaissance of Māori language was derived from the advent of *Te Ataarangi*, a scheme most closely associated with the work of prominent women, Ngoi Pewhairangi and Katrina Mataira. This nonformal learning program's primary goal has been to foster and promote

Maori language through what became known as "the *rakau* method," an inductive approach to learning using everyday objects (such as rakau or sticks) to build up the oral language skills of participants. The heyday for this intervention was the 1980s, coinciding with the blossoming of the kōhanga reo movement. As explained by Hindmarsh (1996, p. 69), the prime function of language enhancement "expanded to include the teaching of life skills, parenting, health, environmental issues, literacy, language research and adult learning." Hence, the life-wide dimensions of learning are again stressed in this approach.

From a broader perspective, a lifelong education system, consisting of Māori education institutions, has been established by Māori, assisted to a modest extent by the public purse. While some of this system is regularized into institutional frameworks and formal classes, there continues a vibrant array of learning possibilities outside this context, those more closely connecting to everyday life, as exemplified by Te Ataarangi. In addition, the Māori Women's Welfare League promotes a full range of learning opportunities for its members, in tune with Māori values.

CONCLUSION

This chapter has been concerned with explaining some of the major elements of Māori knowledge and learning. It has been difficult to disentangle current practices and emergent theory from historical precedents. Clearly, it is foolhardy to present a unitary view of what constitutes Māori knowledge, given the primacy of the tribe and family as locations for most learning in daily life. Knowledge based on the iwi (tribe) is paramount; more general "Māori knowledge" is subsidiary in importance.

The direction of Māori initiatives in recent times has been towards the control of learning by Māori for Māori, yet recognising that there cannot be alienation of Pakeha in the process. The Treaty of Waitangi, and its accompanying principles of partnership, protection, and participation, does provide a framework, albeit contested, for future development. Hopefully, this rendition of Māori learning and knowledge, necessarily selective, does provide some insight into current struggles of Māori for their right to define their own learning priorities while at the same time keeping the state alongside them in their quest for self-determination. In all of this bid for self-determination, it is essential to hold fast to important learning principles handed down through the generations yet be sufficiently proactive to secure new possibilities for the future.

REFERENCES

Bishop, R. & Glynn, T. (2003) *Culture counts: Changing power relations in education.* London: Zed Books.

Doherty, W. (2005). Matauranga Māori (Māori knowledge) and Matauranga Tuhoe (tuhoe knowledge), a holistic lifelong learning approach. Presented at the conference of the Centre for Research in Lifelong Learning, University of Stirling, Scotland, 24 June, 1–25.

Durie, M. H. (2001). *Whaiora: Māori health development.* Auckland: Oxford University Press.

Freire, P. (1972). *Pedagogy of the oppressed.* New York: Continuum Publishing Corporation.

Hemara, W. (2000). *Māori pedagogies—A view from the literature.* New Zealand Council for Educational Research: Wellington.

Hindmarsh, J. (1996) Mapping the field in the 1990s. In J. Benseman, B. Findsen, & M. Scott (Eds.), *The fourth sector: Adult and community education in Aotearoa New Zealand.* (pp.65–76). Palmerston North: The Dunmore Press.

Hohepa, M., McNaughton, S., & Jenkins, K. (1996). Māori pedagogies and the roles of the individual. *New Zealand Journal of Educational Studies,* 31, (1), 29–40.

Hoskins, T. (2005). Māori communities: Critical contexts and pedagogical models for lifelong learning and cultural regeneration. Presented at the conference of the Centre for Research in Lifelong Learning, University of Stirling, Scotland, 24 June, 1–17.

Irwin, J. (1984). *An introduction to Māori religion.* South Australia: Association for the Study of Religions.

Jahnke, H. & Taiapa, J. (1999). Māori research. In C. Davidson &

M. Tolich (Eds.), *Social science research in New Zealand.* (pp. 39–50). Auckland, New Zealand: Pearson Education New Zealand Limited.

Jones, A., Marshall, J., Morris-Matthews, K., Smith, G. H., & Smith, L. T. (1995). (2ⁿᵈ ed.) *Myths and realities: Schooling in New Zealand.* Palmerston North: The Dunmore Press.

Macfarlane, A. H. (2004). The value of Māori ecologies in the study of human development. In W. Drewery & L. Bird (Eds.), *Human development in Aotearoa: A journey through life* (pp. 46–51). Auckland, New Zealand: McGraw-Hill.

Mason, P. (1971) *Patterns of dominance.* London: Oxford University Press.

McCarthy, M. (1996). "He Hinaki Tukutuku: The baited trap. Whare wānanga: Tensions and contradictions in relation to the state." In J. Benseman, B. Findsen, & M. Scott (Eds.), *The fourth sector: Adult and community education in Aotearoa New Zealand.* (pp. 81–94). Palmerston North: The Dunmore Press.

Mead, S. M. (2003). *Tikanga Māori: Living by Māori values.* Wellington: Huia.

Metge, J. (1984). *Learning and teaching: He tikanga Māori.* Wellington, N.Z: Māori and Island Division, Department of Education.

Orbell, M. (1995). *The illustrated encyclopedia of Māori myth and legend.* Christchurch, New Zealand: Canterbury University Press.

Papakura, M. (1986). *Makereti—The old time Māori.* Auckland: New Women's Press.

Pere, R. (1982). *Ako: Concepts of learning in the Māori tradition.* Wellington: *Te kōhanga reo reo* National Trust.

Royal, C. (2004). *Māori and museum practice.* A discussion paper prepared for Te Papa National Services—Te Paerangi (pp. 1–76). Wellington: New Zealand.

Smith, G. H. (1987). *Akonga Māori teaching and learning methodologies.* In Nga Kete Wananga Readers, no. 2, ed. G. H. Smith, Auckland College of Education.

Stewart-Harawira, M. (1997). The impact of the state-welfare relationship on whānau: Implications for education. In M. Olssen, & K. Morris-Matthews (Eds.), *Education policy in New Zealand: The 1990s and beyond.* (pp. 327–345). Palmerston North: The Dunmore Press.

Vygotsky, L. (1978). *Mind in society: The development of higher psychological processes.* London: Harvard University Press.

Walker, R. (1980). Māori adult education. In R. Boshier (Ed.), *Towards a learning society*. (pp.101–120). Vancouver: LearningPress Ltd.

Yates, B. (1996). Striving for tino rangatiratanga. In J. Benseman, B. Findsen, & M. Scott (Eds.), *The fourth sector: Adult and community education in Aotearoa New Zealand*. (pp.95–111). Palmerston North: The Dunmore Press.

Young, M. F. D. (1971). (Ed.). *Knowledge and control: New directions for the sociology of education*. London: Collier Macmillan Publishers.

CHAPTER 6

Buddhist Learning:
A Process to Be Enlightened

Jienshen F. Shih

> All those who are seeking Enlightenment must understand
> this Fourfold Noble Truth. Without understanding this, they
> will wander about interminably in the bewildering maze of
> life's illusions. Those who understand the Fourfold Noble
> Truth are called "the people who have acquired the eyes of
> Enlightenment."
>
> —The Teaching of Buddha

For all Buddhists, to learn is to understand, practice, and
prove the way toward obtaining enlightenment through Buddha's
teachings. The ultimate purpose of being a Buddhist, no matter
one's gender, ethnicity, color, language or occupation, is to learn
to be an enlightened one just like those who have accomplished
this effort in the past. The teachings from the experience of
countless enlightened ones, tested and taught by the Buddha,
and later written down as well as transmitted by his disciples,
have been the guidelines for the followers and learners of Buddhism for thousands of years. Even now, those recorded and preserved teachings are still useful for today's practitioners around
the world.

Buddhism is one of the major and popular religions in the
world. For more than 2500 years, it has spread to different areas
from its original place and added new components along with

its development. Although Buddhism has been regarded as a prominent Eastern religion and philosophy, more and more Western people have recognized, accepted, and even practiced Buddhism. Ironically, as many Eastern people from India, Japan, China, Korea, Hong Kong, Taiwan, and other Asian countries travel to the West to pursue new learning and all kinds of knowledge for individual or organizational benefits, Westerners are at the same time turning to Buddhism and other oriental religions to solve universal or personal problems for a better future. This chapter first introduces the historical background of the Buddha and Buddhism; next, the basic philosophy and concepts are discussed; finally, it concludes with practice and theory in Buddhist learning.

BACKGROUND OF THE
FOUNDER OF BUDDHISM

Knowledge about the founder is helpful to understanding both Buddhism's development and practice. Actually, the historical Buddha, a prince, appropriately demonstrated in his life how Buddhism could be learned and practiced to reach complete freedom, which is the ultimate purpose of learning Buddhism.

The Buddha was born in a small country, Shakya, now a part of India which is at the foothills of the Himalayas. The King, Shuddhodana Gautama and the Queen, Maya, were glad to welcome their only child, Siddhartha, after twenty years' waiting. It was said the Queen became pregnant after she dreamed of a white elephant entering into her womb through the right side of her chest the previous night. However, joy was soon followed by sorrow when the Queen died days after the prince's birth; the child was thus cared for by the Queen's sister, Mahaprajapati. Later, a hermit came to see the baby and predicted the child would become either a great king to subjugate the world or a Buddha if he embraced a religious life (BPIF, 1991). The hermit's forecast was proved years later when the

Prince renounced his secular life and became a religious practitioner.

Prince Siddhartha was married when he was nineteen and lived in luxurious palaces. However, since his youth the Prince had thought about the true meaning of human life. He always pondered what would be the right way for one's life and what was the real goal of a valuable life. These inquiries became so serious that he wanted to find out answers for them. The King noticed his son's sadness and was afraid the Prince would become a religious person as the hermit predicted. Even though the King carefully kept unpleasant things from the Prince to keep him living joyfully, the Prince eventually found another side of life when he met the dead, the sick, the newborn, and the old when he went to walk around the capital city. In these encounters, the Prince found there are prevailing sufferings that no one could avoid. He decided to renounce the secular life and left to seek the truth of human life.

In his journey of truth and meaning seeking, the Prince met and learned from different teachers. In one period, he also practiced asceticism with very little material possessions. After six years, the Prince found asceticism was not useful to real emancipation and gave up the practice. Five fellow ascetics were not satisfied with the Prince's change in behavior and left him. Soon after he meditated under a tree and decided to not leave the seat until he had reached the final enlightenment. After a long and intense meditation, he finally understood the answers he had sought and became a genuine enlightened person.

By his own life, the Prince Siddhartha engaged in a process of meaning seeking which consisted of observations, thinking, practicing, and enlightenment. He demonstrated becoming enlightened is possible and obtainable with his life as a noble prince first, and then a great enlightened figure, a Buddha. In the next forty years, he traveled to different places to teach people how to be an enlightened one. He went to meet the five ascetics and told them what he had realized. They thus became the first disciples of the Buddha. The next section discusses the basic principles of Buddhism, the major product of the Buddha's enlightenment.

THE ORIGINS OF THE BUDDHA'S TEACHING

To some extent, the Buddha's thinking and philosophy denote a mix between two major cultures and their religions which existed before him. On the one hand, the Buddha was the young generation of immigrated Aryans, representing the Aryan Civilization which was closer to the Western cultures. On the other hand, his birthplace was in an Indian area, representing the Indus Valley Civilization (the early Indian Civilization). Santina (1984) compared religions from these two major cultures. Indus Valley Civilization stresses renunciation, meditation, rebirth, karma, and the goal of liberation. The Aryan religion stresses this life, material well-being, wealth, power, fame, and sacrifices as means of achieving these goals. In addition, the Aryan religion also stresses caste—the division of society into social strata—and belief in the authority of the revealed scriptures, the Vedas. Developing between 1500 B.C. and 600 or 500 B.C. was a history of gradual interaction between these two totally different religions. These two religions began to influence, interact, and merge with each other as the Aryans settled across the Indian subcontinent. In Buddha's teaching, he was critically affected by the concepts in these two major civilizations, especially from the Indus Valley religion which includes meditation, renunciation, the concept of rebirth, the notion of karma, and a goal of religious life. Karma is the belief that the deeds or misdeeds in one's present life lead to good or bad consequences in the next life.

THEORY AND PRACTICE

To learn Buddhism, one has to start from getting to know the basic tenets of Buddhism, which include concepts about the life of living beings, relationships among different lives, and relationships between living beings and the physical world. One must also understand how the world has changed and how different worlds have been formed, and how one can cease to go through endless suffering and rebirths and instead proceed toward becoming an emancipated and enlightened one. In addition, Buddhist learning requires not only understanding major philosophies of Buddhism, but also continuously practicing to realize the true meaning of these philosophies. In Buddhist teaching, learning Buddhism means both to learn the teaching of Buddha and to act as a Buddha would act. Thus, understanding the right paths to practice Buddhism is critical to the pursuit of enlightenment. Without appropriate comprehension and practicing, one might waste a lot of time in useless practice and still find little or no progress in learning. To summarize, the core spirit of Buddhist learning is learning to be a free one by following and practicing Buddhist teaching; this is the path toward achieving Buddhahood.

STAGES OF LEARNING BUDDHISM

In Chinese Buddhism, the process of learning is basically divided into three major stages—*wun* (reading and studying), *szu* (thinking and reflection), and *hsiu* (practicing). *Wun* means to study and understand Buddhist teaching from various sources, including different teachers, scriptures, and other media or writings. *Szu* emphasizes thoughtfully and frequently reflecting on learned knowledge from the first stage to obtain a true understanding of Buddhist teaching. The last stage, *hsiu*, is to practice according to what one has understood or realized from the first two stages to become more and more like an enlightened individual. Thus, for a Buddhist, Buddha's teaching is both the material for learning and guidelines for learners to realize and practice the content of the material. Learning for Buddhists actually is an endless process of studying, reflection, and practicing. Studying is the basis to know what the Buddha had gone through and found in his enlightenment. Reflection helps to review the learned teaching and use it as main instructions for further practice. Practicing is the way to experiment and follow the Buddha's teaching for further understanding and advancing individual enlightenment. Hence, learning Buddhism is a journey of continuous studying, practicing, and experiencing Buddhist teachings. The essential requirement for a serious Buddhist learner-practitioner is to study and understand Buddhist basic philosophies.

FOUR NOBLE TRUTHS

When the Buddha attained his enlightenment, his first teaching was the Four Noble Truths. It can be said the Four Noble Truths remain the central jewel common to all teaching of the Buddha (Goldstein, 1994). The first Noble Truth is about impermanence and suffering. There is nothing in this world found as unchanged. Pleasant days are wonderful, but will pass sooner or later. Relationships are changing all the time. Beauty or wealth is cherished but also not everlasting. People usually want good and pleasant things to remain unchanged at least for a long time while wishing to avoid bad situations or people. However, in most cases, what really happens is often different from what people have wished. Thus, desire, ignorance, attachment, and disappointment are aroused and become the causes of never-ending suffering. Impermanence is the basic truth of life and the source of suffering.

Suffering can be divided into two categories—physical and mental. Among physical sufferings, birth is the gateway to the other sufferings. Also, sufferings from birth, aging, sickness, and death are unavoidable (Santina, 1984). The other category is mental sufferings which includes suffering from separation from loved ones, from contact with those one dislikes or those who dislikes one, and from frustrated desire.

The second Noble Truth is to understand the causes of suffering and how these causes result in suffering. The second Noble Truth illustrates how causes are collected, accumulated, and eventually lead to suffering which again becomes the cause of more suffering. In Buddhism, understanding and believing the principle of *cause and effect* are also a fundamental requirement for realizing and practicing Buddha's teaching. Next, the third Noble Truth explains that as long as the causes of suffering are demolished, the sufferings can cease. The last one, the fourth

Noble Truth, shows there are ways to stop the causes of suffering. By following these ways, one can gradually walk away from the causes of suffering and build the possibilities to become enlightened or to achieve so-called *nirvana*.

THE WAY TO ENLIGHTENMENT

The four Noble Truths explain why people are not completely free like enlightened ones, and they also set forth the possibility of reaching the same freedom by understanding and ending the causes of suffering. Based on such an understanding and belief, the Buddha also pointed out the ways to practice to obtain the enlightenment. Basically, the way to accomplish this important effort is called the Noble Eightfold Path—or eight basic paths toward attaining enlightenment. Through these eight practices, one can accumulate the possibility to cease the causes of suffering and gradually approach the state of final emancipation. The Noble Eightfold Path includes Right View, Right Thought, Right Speech, Right Behavior, Right Livelihood, Right Effort, Right Mindfulness, and Right Concentration (BPIF, 1991; Santina, 1984; Takakusu, 1956).

The first path, right view, means to understand teachings of Buddha correctly with a deep belief in the Four Noble Truths. Right thought means the determination not to cherish harmful and indulgent thoughts; instead one should embrace consideration to benefit others. Right thinking reflects the way things are instead of seeing in a distorted way (Nhat Hanh, 1998). Right speech is to avoid any harmful and destructive words to others. Right behavior underlines not to perform bad and dangerous deeds to self and others. Right livelihood in Buddhism stresses making a living by not killing or hurting other beings' lives or safety. Wisdom and understanding have to be integrated into our daily lives to practice the Buddha's teaching (Goldstein, 1987). Right effort is to work and endeavor hard by following right directions. Right mindfulness is the practice of maintaining a pure and clear mind. The last path, right concentration, is to keep the mind right and tranquil for concentration.

These noble paths are called the path to the Cessation of the Cause of Suffering. To any individual, the practice of Buddhism means to find the way to understand the causes of suffering and the methods to stop it completely. In another words, based on the belief that suffering is the obstacle to complete freedom, the determination and practice of the means toward emancipation from suffering become critical and necessary. The Eightfold Path tells how to practice correctly to reduce causes of individual suffering and make enlightenment possible. The following explains these eight core methods for Buddhist practice.

Basically, the Eightfold Path is divided into three categories (or *San Hsueh* in Chinese) as *chieh, ting*, and *hui*. They represent three basic ways of practice: keeping the precepts, practicing concentration of mind, and always acting wisely. *Chieh* requires people to follow right deeds and ethical rules; *ting* means a Buddhist has to concentrate on every moment with a quiet and clear mind; and *hui* is the effect of practice of the first two ways to act wisely and appropriately in different aspects of daily life. A person with wisdom can understand and accept the Four Noble Truths—that is to know the fact of suffering and its nature, the source of suffering, the situation when suffering is ended, and the ways that lead to the end of suffering. In practice, keeping the precepts (or *chieh*) is the base for the other two practices. Without disciplined and ethical living, one would be easily attached to all kinds of desires, emotions, and ignorance that consequently become the causes of suffering.

Therefore, for any serious Buddhist, learning Buddhism starts from practicing and living an ethical life. When people keep the precepts, they easily and naturally obtain concentration of mind. Furthermore, when they are concentrated in mind, it will be less difficult to cultivate wisdom which leads to living wisely in daily life, and is also beneficial toward attaining various levels of enlightenment. Only those who are willing to follow these three ways of practice may be called the disciples of Buddha.

Among the eight paths, right speech, right behavior, and right livelihood belong to *chieh*. Right mindfulness and right concentration are both practices of *ting*. With regard to *hui* practice, right view and right thought are in this category. Fi-

Eight Noble Paths	Three Ways of Practice
Right Speech Right Behavior Right Livelihood	Good conduct, morality (Shila, *Chieh*)
Right Mindfulness Right Concentration	Mental development or meditation (Samadhi, *Ting*)
Right View Right Thought	Wisdom or insight (Prajna, *Hui*)
Right Effort (the drive to practice and accomplish the other seven paths)	

Figure 6.1 Relationship between the Eight Noble Paths and the Three Ways of Practice

nally, right effort is the critical drive to practice and accomplish the other seven paths. A comparison between the Eight Noble Paths and the three ways of practice are shown in Figure 6.1. Based on the above explanation, it could be said the purpose of Buddhist learning is to become an enlightened one while the methods of learning are various and inclusive. To sum up, the practice of Buddhism is to achieve the purpose of pursuing complete freedom or so-called Buddhahood.

MIDDLE-WAY PRACTICE— A BALANCED LEARNING

A Buddhist has to keep the learning in a balanced condition to make the practice of pursuing the final freedom possible. In Buddha's teaching, he frequently pointed out that a good practitioner should not go too fast or too slowly. Some practitioners of his days thought that one has to renounce all the basic needs and enter into an ascetic practice to become enlightened. However, the Buddha demonstrated himself that living in a balanced way, without too much luxury or too little care for a person's need, is helpful to keeping a healthy body and a peaceful mind. A stable condition will further benefit the development of individual wisdom and move one a step closer to enlightenment. The Eightfold Path is the practice for realizing and carrying out the core teachings of Buddha.

PRACTICE IN EVERYDAY LIFE

In Buddhist practice, especially in Chinese Buddhism, learning happens in all moments and places. Historically, Buddhism was spread over different areas by Buddhist disciples. When Buddhism was introduced to a new place, it would be adjusted to and integrated with the local culture and customs to enhance its acceptance by the local people. Buddhism in China absorbed Chinese culture and became a unique Chinese Buddhism which later was transmitted to East Asia such as Korea, Japan, Taiwan, and other neighboring countries. In China, Buddhism was welcomed and received with great courtesy by the royalty. Later, these early missionaries from South Asia began to build monasteries and recruit more people to attend the practice. A large monastery is like a community with everyone responsible for an assigned position or task (*tzu-shih*) and these positions cover different kinds of work in a monastery (Shih, 1997).

Tzu-shih, in Chinese Buddhism, is part of a monastic's practice and it is believed that one could achieve the purpose of reducing suffering and accumulating merits by being responsible to one's *tzu-shih*. In addition, taking meals, sleeping, or walking are all part of Buddhist practice. In Buddhism, one practices mindfulness by doing everything with attention in daily life. There are abundant stories in Chinese Buddhism that some monastics obtained great enlightenment by just working diligently in the kitchen or doing labor work for years. In Buddhist teaching, keeping a calm and clear mind, or right mindfulness, is critical to developing true wisdom toward stopping suffering. Focusing on one's current work and maintaining a pleasant attitude in serving other people are helpful to diminishing desires and increasing merits toward self purification and illumination. Theoretically, Buddhists need to go through innumerous lives to accumulate enough merits to become closer to the final goal.

TEACHING AND LEARNING IN
THE BUDDHIST TRADITION

In Buddhism, teachers make use of scriptures, stories, and numerous dialogues between the Buddha and his disciples that are easily understood and close to the needs of the learners. When the Buddha organized the *Sangha* (the community for monastics), he required all members in the Sangha to bag offerings from the village people every morning. After that, all monastics would share the food together, including those who were too old or too sick. After this single meal of the day, the Buddha and all his disciples would sit down and one of them would ask the Buddha a question. The Buddha would answer the question and solve the confusion the disciples might have had. These dialogues happened very often in the Buddha's teaching. These dialogues were memorized and retold after the Buddha passed away. Even now, these dialogues can be read again and one can imagine a joyful scene of a teacher and his students sharing some questions. After the questions were answered, according to the scriptures, all the members were satisfied with the teaching and some of them even reached different degrees of enlightenment.

Such dialogues not only happened in the location of a fixed place, they also frequently happened in the middle of their walking between different villages. One time, when the Buddha saw a pile of white bones, he asked his disciples who had the knowledge about these bones. From there, he began to tell them the stories about those white bones. Eventually, the disciples understood the relationships between people in different generations and expressed gratitude to one's parents of previous lives. Dialogues like this became the stories transferred to Buddhist followers. Today, Buddhist practitioners still can read and meditate on these stories to obtain new understanding and insights in their practice.

In addition to dialogues, the Buddha also frequently used

fables for his teaching. A fable would be used to explain some Buddhist philosophy such as *karma, the Four Noble Truths,* or *cause-and-effect.* Fables were usually told like an attractive and interesting story. Through fables, people could understand some concepts easily and apply them to one's practice. These fables also were passed down to future generations. They are appropriate for both adults and children. It is easy to find a scripture called *Pai Yu Ching* (The Sutra of One Hundred Fables) in any popular bookstore in Taiwan. Some of these interesting stories even have been used for children's ethical education or for material for artistic creations. One of these fables is as follows:

> Once the Buddha told a story about a person who had two hundred and fifty cows. One day a tiger came to the farm and ate one of the cows. The farmer thought "I originally had two hundred and fifty cows and that counts as a complete number. Now, I lost one of the cows and the number is not complete any more, so what is the use for me to keep these cows?" Thus, he drove all the cows to a side of a deep hole and pushed all the cows into the hole to kill all of them. The Buddha, after recounting this fable, told his disciples that normal people are just like this farmer. When one follows two hundred and fifty vows and incidentally violates one of them, this person should repent of his fault. However, instead he says: "Since I have spoiled one vow, I am not complete any more, what is the use for me to keep other vows?" This is just like the farmer who killed all the cows just because one of them was eaten by the tiger.

Fables like these helped the disciples realize how to follow the teaching of the Buddha in a vigorous way.

It can be said that in the Buddha's teaching, he liked to use different ways to make people understand concepts of Buddhism. In some ways, he was not only a great religious founder, but also a skillful and creative adult educator. In Buddha's teaching, there are different ways of interaction between the teacher and the disciples, and raising questions is one of most used ways displayed in the scriptures.

Current monastics still used these stories for their learning according to a study by this chapter's author (Shih, 1997). One of the female practitioners interviewed in this study said she frequently read these stories in the scriptures and reflected on the meaning of them. New insights from these stories helped her find methods to solve problems met in her work. This means records of the Buddha's teaching benefited not only his disciples at his time, but also followers of today and future generations.

CONCLUSION

For all serious Buddhists, the ultimate purpose of learning of a person is to become an enlightened one. A person learning Buddhism needs to understand basic philosophies of Buddha's teaching before commencing any practice. In Buddhism, learning and practicing are two sides of one thing and both are pointed to the same goal. The learning covers every aspect of human life. Basically, all learning is divided into three categories, *chieh, ting, hui. Chieh* is to keep an ethical lifestyle and is the foundation for the others, *ting* is mindful in every moment, and *hui* is living and acting wisely. Living an ethical and disciplined life makes it more possible to develop true mindfulness and wisdom. The process of learning begins with understanding the Four Noble Truths. Based on this belief, one follows the practice of the Eightfold Path to gradually walk toward the achievement of enlightenment. Buddhist learning is a process of endless practice which is not only lifelong but also necessarily extended to innumerous lives. Learning to be Buddhist is a balanced endeavor. Middle-way practice is most beneficial to Buddhist learning. Learning also happens and is counted in every moment and every facet of daily life. By concentrating and being mindful in doing or dealing with everything, one is doing the right practice and walking toward the right direction. Evaluation of learning for a Buddhist consists of reflecting and checking whether one has better realized the Four Noble Truths and become freer from suffering. Buddhism is actually continuous learning and a whole-human practice for a final and complete freedom—Enlightenment.

REFERENCES

The Buddhist Promoting International Foundation, YMBA Report. (1991). *The teaching of Buddha*. Seattle, WA: Author.

Goldstein, J. (1987). *The experience of insight: A simple and direct guide to Buddhist meditation*. Boston, MA: Shambhala Dragon.

Goldstein, J. (1994). *Insight meditation: The practice of freedom*. Boston, MA: Shambhala Dragon.

Nhat Hanh, Thich. (1998). *The heart of the Buddha's teaching: Transforming suffering into peace, joy, and liberation*. New York: Broadway.

Santina, P. D. (1984). *Fundamentals of Buddhism*. Carmel, NY: The Institute for Advanced Studies of World Religions, Chuang Yen Monastery.

Shih, J. F. (1997). *How religious professionals learn: An exploration on learning by Buddhist professionals in Taiwan*. Unpublished doctoral dissertation. University of Wisconsin-Madison.

Takakusu, J. (1956). *The essentials of Buddhist philosophy* (3rd ed.). Honolulu, HI: University of Hawaii.

CHAPTER 7

African Indigenous Knowledge: The Case of Botswana

Gabo Ntseane

As we enter the third millennium where we live in a global village, Africa is trying to locate itself in this new situation by reimagining and reinventing itself along certain ideologies and philosophical lines. One of the more recent manifestations of the search for meaning and identity has been the concept of African indigenous knowledge. Given the legacy of colonialism and Western knowledge imperialism, an acute awareness has developed within nonacademic and academic circles to reclaim and explore the core essence of African indigenous knowledge and its contribution to humanity and science. In fact, the ideas expressed have generated a form of dialogue among scholars reflecting on the relationship between traditional versus modern education.

Education and learning are not recent interventions in many African ethnic groups because they are an integral part of the life and have therefore always been there. Research on African traditional education (Magagula & Mazibuko, 2004; Mautle, 2001; Morolong, 1996; Ocitti, 1988) reveals that in traditional societies, education, learning, and training had their own specific principles, methods, and social institutional arrangements. For example, learning by doing instead of writing has been a prominent principle in the education of many ethic groups for training intellect, imparting technical skills as well as moral values. However, a closer look at current practices in schools and adult literacy classes easily shows that both are acting strongly against this very important principle of African pedagogy. In fact there is preference for what Ocitti (1988, p. 1) calls "bookish memorization and copy-copy mentality." This chapter gives examples that are testimony that in the African context that is characterized by an oral instead of a book-reading culture you don't pass useful information through books because learning will simply not happen.

The literature (Gumede, 1996; Lange, 1997) also shows that a major principle of African indigenous knowledge systems is that to learn is to live usefully and happily with one's family, with one's community, with one's society, and with the spirits of one's ancestors, hence the importance of the words *botho* in Setswana or *úbuntu* in Zulu. Although these words are from two different languages and two different countries, their literal translation is "humanism of human beings collectively." Another distinguishing feature of African indigenous education is that informality, collective learning, oral mode of instruction, and acquisition of revealed knowledge through the processes of dreams and visions are common instructional methods. This chapter gives examples of how these training methods are used in Botswana indigenous knowledge learning situations.

Given that current adult education practices in Africa have overlooked some of these important principles of African pedagogy, this chapter defines African indigenous knowledge. An emphasis on the metaphors from the Botswana indigenous knowledge system shows how knowledge is buried in the proverbs. The chapter also discusses the academic value or relevance of how core curriculum matters are treated in the indigenous knowledge of the Botswana system. Finally, the chapter advocates for a creative adult education practice that makes it possible for Africans to modernize their traditions but also at the same time allows them to traditionalize modernity.

EDUCATION AND INDIGENOUS KNOWLEDGE: AN AFRICAN PERSPECTIVE

Education from an African perspective is in part an instrument of socializing people to their cultural heritage and value systems. According to Magagula and Mazibuko (2004) education is expected to enable African people to "appreciate and understand their history; way of life and cultural identity; who they are; where they come from; where they are now; where they will be tomorrow and how they will get there" (p. 1). Education or lifelong learning is a collective activity that is supposed to help the individual in the collective to reach the highest level of critically important values to the African's way of life such as *botho* or humanism. By being *botho* or behaving with dignity (i.e., distinction, honesty, integrity, and trustworthiness) among the collective, the individual then becomes part of an empowered group of people who are honest, accommodating, sharing, responsible citizens who respect the young and the old.

In the African context the opposite of *botho* (or humanity) is selfishness, greediness, and self-centeredness. The values of *botho* or *úbuntu* have always been part of the African culture that has been transmitted from generation to generation through what is called cultural or indigenous education. Cunningham (1997) conceives *úbuntu* as an African worldview of philosophy of life that incorporates values of personhood, humanness, morality, honesty, and concern for the social good. He further observes that because of the emphasis on materialistic and instrumental value systems in the school curriculum, the values of *úbuntu* have taken the back stage in the education curriculum. As a result of education systems that neglect the African philosophy of life, it can be argued that one of the major conflicts in Africa and globally has been lack of understanding, appreciation, and tolerance of other cultures and way of life of other people.

Adult Education

Beginning with the definition of adult education by Linderman, inherent in the mission and tradition of adult education as a discipline is that individualism was not the initial agenda for adult education; rather, a social function was the basis of adult education. According to Briton (1996) adult education is a cultural practice with moral and political responsibility that reaches far beyond the walls of the classroom. This implies that good adult education practice should draw attention to processes going on in the group or society as adult educators are social reformers. Another important principle or philosophy of adult education is that personal knowledge is a source of knowledge. In fact Welton (1995) argues that the role of adult education is to assist adults in their construction of their own knowledge about their life and this should be done through participatory research.

Both the African definition and the mission of Adult education seem to emphasize the need for useful knowledge. Useful knowledge according to Segall (2002, p. 56) has to "enable an understanding of human experience, enhance respect and help people to deal critically and creatively with the world in order to change it." Ideally, if adult education is to contribute to useful knowledge, it has to act as a vehicle of cultural and social change by validating and enhancing other disadvantaged groups' experiences.

While the mission and tradition of adult education seem relevant to the understanding of the concept of education from the African perspective, current adult education practice is perceived as lacking ability to respond to the needs and interests of indigenous communities in Africa. The major shortcoming of adult education in Africa has been that it elevates technical rationality over other forms of knowledge, human thought, and discourses. Examples include its preoccupation with service to and the perpetuation of economic character of the modern society; its serving as an agent of social control for the state, and its failure to defend and preserve indigenous people's cultural integrity. According to Fafunwa (1971) African indigenous education emphasized social responsibility, job orientation, political participation, and appreciation of spiritual and moral values.

African Indigenous Knowledge

African indigenous knowledge was defined as a "locally-based knowledge that is generated through a systematic process of observing the local environment, experimenting with solutions and the re-adoption of previously identified solutions to changing environmental factors" (P. Brouwer, quoted in Morolong, 1996, p. 3). The principle guiding the provision of indigenous African education as Adeyinka (1991) clearly points out was functionalism. Its purpose was to prepare the African child for adult life and peaceful death. This suggests that indigenous knowledge from the African perspective is knowledge that has enabled the locals to respond to their everyday realities and experiences, hence it is locally based.

In African contexts, the indigenous knowledge system is traditional/customary education whose aims are:

a. To preserve the cultural heritage of the extended family, clan and the tribe.

b. To adapt members of the new generation to their physical environment and teach them how to control and use it.

c. To explain to them that their own future, and that of their community depends on the understanding and perpetuation of the institution, laws, language and values inherited from the past (Datta, 1984, p. 9).

Acquisition and Sharing of African Indigenous Knowledge

Knowledge and practices are empirical and based on continuous observation, imitation, and continuous practice. Traditional education involved all the human senses while emphasizing a hands-on approach. For instance, children participated in the social process of adult activities by identification and imitation, learned through observing adult practices and emulating them.

Skill acquisition dominated traditional education and these skills were generally acquired through observation by the learners. Datta (1984) posits that the content of African customary education grew out of the physical and more importantly, the social situation. That traditional education in Africa is socially determined is clearly reflected in the main characteristic attributes of customary education identified by Monyatsi (2004) as:

a. African traditional societies laid a heavy stress on informal instruction as far as general education was concerned.

b. Compared to modern education, customary education in Africa was marked with limited specialized training.

c. It also lacked a distinct category of professionalism, such as a full-time teacher, as every member of the society has a part to play.

This knowledge is imparted to the youth through a phased childhood and adolescence. It encourages children to engage in *participatory education* through ceremonies and rituals (associated with rain-making, sowing and harvesting of crops, pregnancies, birth, name giving, twins, sickness and death, purification rites as well as those associated with new shrines, etc.), spiritual work such as weaving and farming, recreation work such as dancing, and intellectual training such as storytelling and poetry. For instance, storytelling is the traditional means to transfer ethical values through the generations.

My childhood phase is characterized by memories of stories from my grandmothers and my friend's grandmothers in the village. These stories illustrated ways of the past that tacitly conveyed values to the young. I still remember that my grandmothers' methods and styles of narration were expressed in a performance quality and this captured my attention. Practical forms of storytelling such as singing and gestures were manipulated in different voices. Because the audience participation is important, my grandmother insisted that listeners of her stories had to acknowledge by replying "*Ëee*" for yes and "*mm*" for ok, with a sharp intake of breath (mmh). This knowledge is stored in cultural and religious beliefs, taboos, folklore, or myths as much as in the individual's practical experience.

Herding of goats and cattle, farming, and hunting provided scenarios for boys that are today found in the form of libraries, laboratories and classrooms, or today's educational tours or excursions. It was during such activities that they learned the names of plants, trees, animals, and insects as well as their uses and dangers. These were done under the watchful, experienced, and sometimes professional eyes of the fathers and uncles. The kitchens, forests where firewood was collected, river ponds where water was fetched, fields where crops were harvested, all provided for the girls who were also under the watchful, educated experienced, and professional eyes of the mothers and aunts, including grandmothers, most of whom were professional midwives in their own right. What were inculcated into the young people were not only skills but acceptable behaviors and attitudes. By preferring utilitarian to hierarchical or theoretical concepts, knowledge is more easily shared. For example, even children are considered teachers as attested to in these proverbs; *"Don't throw away weeds found in a child's wild vegetable harvest."* The idea here is that what you see as weeds could actually be new knowledge. Another proverb that demonstrates the value of children's ideas and experience in knowledge construction is *"If you want to quickly identify an adult's intelligence, study their offspring's actions."* This means that the knowledge we give to our children comes out even more refined because the African indigenous knowledge's emphasis on the learners' active participation triggers creativity, assertiveness, and clarity.

Mode of Instruction

Because informality is one of the distinguishing features of African indigenous education, there has been a tendency among some people to jump to the conclusion that teachers never existed in pre-colonial African societies. In oral societies like those in Africa, every normal person besides being required to be a productive worker also played the double role of learner and teacher, but all in respect and mutual responsibility that guides teaching and learning in a humanist context. For instance, prior to the European influence, the system of indigenous formal education in Africa was purely oral. The learners were simply told things and made to repeat the actions of their instructors and the curriculum emphasized survival skills applicable in the learner's immediate environment.

A unique form of formal instruction in the traditional African education is that of acquisition of revealed knowledge through the processes of dreams and visions. For example, many herbalists in the past and even today in Botswana claim that the secrets of their medicines and how they should be administered were communicated to them mainly through dreams.

It is clear from the above that African indigenous knowledge systems emphasized practical over theoretical modes of skills acquisition and knowledge generation. Indigenous knowledge was generated through practical means and emulation of elders by youngsters was the main mode of learning. Tribal legends and proverbs were told and retold by the evening fireside, and through them much was transmitted to the younger generation and kept alive. This is emphasized by Datta (1984, p. 3) who declares that "Riddles were used to test the children's judgment, myths to explain the origins of the tribe and the genesis of man. Oral tradition, narrated with care and repetition, also constituted the African child's learning."

INITIATION SCHOOLS AS A FORM OF INDIGENOUS EDUCATION

In Botswana as in other parts of Africa, the modern form of education was introduced among Batswana in the 1840s by European missionaries of various churches (Catholic, Dutch Reform, Methodist, Seven Day Adventist, and Protestant). Prior to the missionaries, the only formal education (more intense face-to-face instruction) that existed was the initiation schools for adolescent boys and girls. These traditional schools were separated according to gender, i.e., *Bogwera* for boys and *Bojale* for girls. The entry age for girls was the early teens or any time after reaching the age of puberty and for boys it was the late teens— 17 and above (Brown, 1921, p. 5).

Curriculum

The curricula of the two schools had common subject matter but also had gender specific content. The main goal of the

initiation school education was to prepare the youth for adulthood. It equipped learners with skills they would require to lead
a productive adult life in their society. According to Mautle
(2001), the youth were equipped only with time-tested skills
developed by their ancestors. Conformity to societal norms,
mores, and ways of doing things was also instilled in them. This
is best illustrated by Brown's observation that neophytes were
taught

> reverence for antiquity, aversion to change, conformity to tradi-
> tional custom and the completeness of Sechuana and woman-
> hood as embodied in the circumcision rites. A man must do as
> his forbears did, speak as they spoke. . . . Things remain they
> don't pass away, and they don't change. (1921, p. 15)

The emphasis on conformity in the Botswana indigenous
knowledge, in particular, was common to other initiation schools
in Southern Africa and beyond in the continent. Writing about
women's initiation in other parts of Africa, Lincoln (1981) has
noted that a woman's initiation was

> a ritual enacted by a society as a whole—to preserve the social
> status quo—it serves only to introduce an individual into a so-
> ciety as society already exists—the desired result of the ritual is
> to make a girl willing and ready to assume the traditional place
> of a woman as defined within a given culture. (p. 106)

The common curriculum included the following:

a. The learner's physiological changes and entry into adulthood.

b. History of their people (imparted largely through praise or
   factual poems).

c. Cosmology.

d. Heir responsibilities in society, which differed according to
   gender.

e. Sex education.

f. Socially desirable attitudes (imparted through riddles, puzzles,
   and proverbs).

The specialist curriculum for boys included hunting and fighting skills. This was critical because there were no standing armies and in times of war all men would be called upon to constitute the army. Curriculum for girls included matters concerning womanhood such as child-rearing, domestic and agricultural activities, and behavior toward men. Obedience was taught largely through informing boys and girls about the consequences of disobedience. For example, if the boys were disobedient they would *"feel the law of the vultures"* or *"be eaten by the buffaloes."* They were also told about good rewards for obedience. For example, one who had been obedient would be commended or praised when he entered the initiation. Lessons on survival skills such as agricultural activities, fighting, and self-defense tactics were taught through practical skills under the supervision of instructors. Craft work and physical training were also part of the initiation school curriculum as well as sex education and spiritual education.

Assessment. In the absence of literacy, indigenous education was not an education geared toward passing any particular examination. Instead, it was an education for life adjustment and acceptable living. Mautle (2001) observed that assessment of indigenous formal education in Botswana (i.e., *Bogwera* and *Bojale* initiation schools) included making initiates rehearse the core lessons or knowledge acquired and performing group tasks as regiments or cohorts. A positive assessment was related to honesty and preserving the molding of the individual's character.

In the case of Botswana indigenous education, real graduation occurred only after a group of these young people had successfully (as a cohort) initiated the cohort that followed theirs. As a collective the group that has done well would receive presents of cows from the community members at a special welcome community ceremony organized for the graduating cohort. In addition to the presents this graduating cohort would be given a regiment name strategically picked from the needs or current situation of the society. It is important to mention that presents were not given to the individuals but to the new regiment to use for a community development project that would be associated with their collective achievement. Alternatively, the cohort could use their graduation present to organize a feast in order to appease the spirits of the ancestors for their unconditional protection. Another important contribution of African indigenous learning experience is that the instruction approaches introduce one to a lifelong process. The next section demonstrates how the indigenous knowledge experience is in fact a lifelong learning journey.

BOTSWANA INDIGENOUS KNOWLEDGE AS LIFELONG LEARNING

Although its content is mostly contextualized, however, the lessons and modes of instruction demonstrate that indigenous knowledge is learning throughout life. The use of proverbs, wisdom, dreams, visions and other epistemological tenets in the Botswana indigenous knowledge discussed in this section attest to the fact that it is also lifelong learning.

The Use of Proverbs

Senior men and women are expected to know and use proverbs in discussing important and difficult matters. A good speaker in an African society is one who does not make direct simple statements but one who substitutes and punctuates points with the use of proverbs, idioms, and similes. Proverbs are thus believed to distinguish between deliberations of young men and women from those of wise and knowledgeable adults. For example, the Setswana proverb *"Motho ga a itsiwe e se naga"* (It is easier for a man to know the veld than to know another man) reflects the deep knowledge and understanding of nature. The traditional farmer does not only depend on nature for his food but also uses it to predict and assess the success of the farming for every season.

This keen interest and attentiveness to nature has thus equipped many elderly people who grew up in the rural areas with an inherent knowledge and understanding of nature. Most of them can tell just by an abundance or lack of certain plants that there will either be a lot of rain or little rain that year. They can also tell by the color of the grass and leaves what season it is or by the shade of the sky when it will rain. This proverb is also used to warn children against strangers. For example, when a parent uses it instead of saying to the child, "To you child, I say be careful, some of the people who come to you are not friends or have good intentions," the parent would say, "*A person is not known like the veld.*"

Botswana is also an egalitarian society in which emphasis is placed on mutual coexistence and a sense of collective belonging. A number of proverbs emphasize collective responsibility and cooperation among members of the society as illustrated in the following:

- "*Kgetsi ya tsie e kgonwa ke go tshwaraganelwa*" (A bag of locusts becomes lighter when it is held by many people).
- "*Mokoduwe go tsosiwa o o itekang*" (You lift an old cow that is trying to get up) meaning help is given to those who are making an effort to help themselves.
- "*Se tshwarwa ke nja bedi gase thata*" (A job that is done by many people is quickly accomplished).
- "*Kgosi ke kgosi ka batho ba gagwe*" (The ultimate internal sovereignty in a native community lies in the people and not in the Chief). It is by the consent of their general will that anyone becomes a chief.

The images from nature and behavior of animals are used in proverbs as teaching aids about life by which people can learn to organize and rationalize their lives. Proverbs are effective as a way of communication because each possesses a structured relationship in concrete and easily apprehended terms. Furthermore, in Botswana a proverb is not only an effective instrument for transmitting ideas but it is a kind of oral record of the total wisdom of a people from the past, influencing the present and aiding a projection of the future.

Wisdom

In Africa and Botswana in particular, wisdom is an important epistemological tenet. For example, a look at one of the social and life skill tenets, namely the *reproductive tenet* that has been passed on from one generation to another using narrative epistemology, shows the power of wisdom in the African indigenous knowledge construction and acquisition.

Reproductive education has always been a secret in the indigenous ways of life. In spite of this, some information that was passed to females during reproductive training demonstrates other ways of knowing in Botswana culture. A pregnant woman was told not to eat eggs since the egg yolk would block the mouth of the womb during labor and this might result in complications during delivery. The rationale for not eating eggs was to guard against edema (swelling), proteinuira (protein in the urine), and hypertension (EPH) and weight gain during pregnancy. Given that there were no modern doctors or equipment to assist in highly complicated deliveries, the elderly women wanted to discourage weight gain since the fetus might grow big and require a caesarian at birth.

Once the baby was born, certain beliefs and practices were and are still being observed today in an effort to provide health education prevention of certain ailments. For instance, a newborn baby and its mother are usually isolated from the rest of the family and community for between three and six months depending on whether it was the first child or it was an experienced mother. For example, it is believed that a newborn baby should not be exposed (i.e., spend most of the time outdoors) because the air outside is likely to have more bacteria. Therefore, instead of just telling people to observe this health prevention method, there is a traditional belief that a child who is exposed will develop *mopakwana*, meaning that the child might be infected by germs that can cause physical disability.

Another health prevention practice is that sexually active adults are also not allowed to see a newborn baby who is still confined to the house. Again, to ensure that this is adhered to, there is an indigenous knowledge concept called *maoto a molelo* or the belief that sexually active adults' feet are too hot for the baby. Furthermore, in the Setswana culture everybody who holds a newborn (0–3 months) baby has to wash hands before holding the baby. This is another cultural practice that reenforces the need to protect the baby from infections. All this education was and is still done to protect both the baby and the new mother from infectious diseases. Thus indigenous epistemology also addressed health prevention.

Through these reproductive practices and beliefs, we see wisdom as an epistemological tenet. Wisdom is relevant for reducing the rate of infection from the people to the most vulnerable such as a new baby and its mother. On a simplistic view, it appears to be common sense, but it is wisdom based on strong indigenous knowledge and a strong relationship with the environment, and the subjects subscribe to it. In fact, there are proverbs in place to reenforce the role of wisdom in the African indigenous epistemology, e.g. *"You cannot have an old head on young shoulders"* meaning that a young person cannot have the wisdom and experience of an older person. The reproductive skill tenet used as an example above, attests to the fact that the theorizing some of us do as scientists is not different in kind from anyone else's or from what we do as laypersons.

The Use of Dreams and Visions

A unique form of formal instruction in the traditional African education is that of acquisition of revealed knowledge through the processes of dreams and visions. This is reflective of the Botswana culture's perception of the human, the physical, and the spiritual world as one. As a Motswana (i.e., a Botswana citizen), I see myself or identity in relation to the earth (*lefatshe*) and the spirits of my deceased ancestors (*badimo*). As Preece and Ntseane (2003) observed, the meaning of an obvious and universal health problem such as HIV/AIDS differs depending on the context of the illness. For example, it can be associated with the unhealthy relations of the patient with his or her family, community, or ancestral spirits. As Chilisa (2001) cautions, there is need to avoid the educator bias in dismissing these realities and creating an error of sameness with the First World definitions and knowledge base.

Furthermore, many herbalists and traditional spiritual healers both in the past and today in Africa and in Botswana claim that the secret of their medicines and how they should be administered were communicated to them mainly through dreams (i.e., facts revealed in your sleep). So, unlike the modern doctor at the government hospital or clinic who might suggest a blood test or some specimen to take to the laboratory, it is not uncommon for a traditional doctor to request that a patient return the following day because he or she, as the herbalist or spiritual healer, has to sleep on the problem so that the *badimo* (spirits of the ancestors) of the patient can instruct the healer on how to heal the patient and with what herbs. This is important in traditional medicine because the ancestors of the patient could reveal through a dream that it is time for the patient's spirit to join them so what is needed is for the patient's family to appease them (spirits) so that the patient's death will be peaceful. These are two examples of Africa's acquisition of knowledge through dreams.

Similarly, knowledge can be through visions, that is, being able to see underlying factors about something or somebody such as their ailments, thoughts, fears, experiences, and even their future. For example, my deceased grandmother who was also a traditional midwife was known in the community for being able to see the sex of the unborn baby by looking at the eyes of a pregnant woman. Modern doctors provide the same information by using the help of technology (scan). It is not uncommon in Africa for people (regardless of age) to predict what will happen in the near future by reading their subconscious visions such as repeatedly getting flashbacks of some experience (e.g., a car accident, deceased community leaders or ancestors) and concluding that something bad is about to happen to somebody they know. Because such indigenous knowledge acquisition methods as dreams and visions are marginalized by the West, Africans are likely to question *any* knowledge from a Western perspective. Therefore, the extent to which Africans make connections with scientific knowledge will depend on the extent to which they feel their own positions are accepted and understood. So there is need for adult education to recognize values outside the dominant perspective and to accept that the oppressed and unrecognized voices can have epistemological privilege.

AFRICAN INDIGENOUS KNOWLEDGE TODAY

Academic knowledge and the science or art of knowing in Botswana can be traced back to the advent of Western education. In particular, three distinct periods are discernable in the history of Western education in the whole of Africa.

Three Periods of Western Influence

These three periods are the pre-colonial which was an era of traditional education indigenous to the local inhabitants. In the colonial period, the education system entirely depended on the colonizer. An evident characteristic is that teaching methods departed from the indigenous ways of teaching and learning to the introduction of the Western culture such as reading materials from and about the colonizer's country and culture. The post-colonial period is an era where education practitioners are faced with the ills of Western education. For example, in Botswana, the emphasis of the National Commission of Education (1976 and the revised one in 1997) placed an emphasis on the use of relevant and effective education values and methods. However, relevant to this chapter is the observation that indigenous knowledge is seldom included in the current teaching methods.

Reconstruction of African Indigenous Knowledge

Although this chapter advocates for the African indigenization of adult education curriculum, it by no means advocates for a complete uprooting of the other cultural aspects in the current curriculum that are good. It has to be acknowledged that African indigenous knowledge systems need to be reconstructed so that only what is good is adapted. For instance, in the reconstruction of indigenous knowledge for an effective HIV/AIDS prevention strategy in Botswana, some of the traditional sex education models will have to be revised or discarded. The gender inequality practices in sexuality issues in particular have to go if every human being is to participate in the fight against HIV/AIDS.

One would argue that even in the phase of globalization, to be useful, knowledge has to be contextualized. This is critical in my view because individuals, organizations, and communities must contextualize the information that they receive from within and outside their own environments, if that knowledge is to be used productively to solve their own problems. Cognizant that information and communication technology (ICT) have made knowledge production and exchange easier and further enhanced the methodologies of knowledge discovery, it is important to reconstruct African indigenous knowledge so that it too can benefit from the new learning developments.

The formal Western type of educational system currently offered in Africa has left out most of the forms of African indigenous knowledge systems, although they are still being practiced especially in the rural areas. This marginalized status is a result of a number of historical processes that viewed such knowledge systems as uncivilized, barbaric, and archaic. First, the contact, conquest, colonization, and other forms of association that nurtured imperialism led to the loss of the official recognition of the learning principles and practices of African indigenous knowledge.

Second, the pressure of modernization and cultural diffusion threatened indigenous knowledge systems, thus leaving them scattered, isolated, decimated, and dislocated. In fact, what indigenous people saw as useful knowledge was undermined and rejected. With reference to the missionaries, the church was used as a vehicle for promoting Western education in the name of salvation. For example, the early church focused on teaching reading, writing, and Christianity. Part of the reason was that colonial governments required local clerks and junior officials to know how to read the Bible.

Third is the importance of knowledge to societies' economic systems, because it is becoming increasingly obvious even in Africa that money is a commodity whose driving force is knowledge acquisition. As Gathu (2003) observed, the current trend worldwide today is to talk of a "knowledge-based economy." A knowledge-based economy is an economy in which production, distribution, and the use of knowledge is the main driver of growth, wealth creation, and employment across all societies. Therefore, within the African indigenous knowledge systems, the historical production and survival skill training focus has to be analyzed in relation to these new economic trends.

DEBATES ON INDIGENOUS KNOWLEDGE'S SURVIVAL IN THE FACE OF WESTERNIZATION/GLOBALIZATION

Critics of African indigenous knowledge have argued that it is difficult to develop African indigenous systems for several reasons. First, they argue that such knowledge is closed, unsystematic, subjective, and lacking in analytical aspects. This is debatable because the value of any system of education is not that it should be shared with others, but rather it should suit or meet the learning needs of the society or nations for which it is intended.

Second, others have argued that indigenous knowledge is difficult to conceptualize because it builds on experiences. For instance, the interpretation of a proverb clearly shows that the meaning of the proverb depends on a context (i.e., on who and when it is used) and on the interaction between the speaker and the participants. In a way the context in which a proverb is used determines its function. While diversity of indigenous knowledge should be acknowledged, the reality is that although the systems and models are different, a closer analysis will also show "common understandings" across the knowledge systems.

Third, some critics believe that indigenous knowledge develops on the basis of insights that do not fall within strictly established methods of science, which often seeks universalization. For example, Western epistemology discredits narrative as a way of knowing that is not verifiable, not scientific, and that cannot be validated. I would also argue that indigenous epistemology that is based on narrative in an oral culture like mine (African) is a powerful way of knowing since it connects to the experiences of the subjects and has direct relevance to the environment and social groups. Overall, it is clear that the stifling of the advancement of the African indigenous knowledge has led to the influx and comparative advantage of Western science and technologies.

IDEAS FOR THE AFRICAN INDIGENIZATION OF ADULT EDUCATION

In the context of globalization, adult education like feminist education has the opportunity to become a space for alternative knowledge traditions. Both the indigenization and the modernization of adult education curricular in educational institutions could be a good start in helping young African generations to learn, understand, and appreciate African value systems, norms, beliefs, and practices parallel to other society's education paradigms, including the dominant Western perspectives. It has been argued in other forums that one of the major conflicts in Africa and globally has been lack of understanding, appreciation, and tolerance of other cultures and way of life of other people. This situation can be explained by an emphasis on materialistic and instrumental value system in the school curriculum as the African values of *botho* (humanity in the collective) have taken the back stage in education curriculum. The following are some of the ideas for the African indigenization of adult education practice:

• *Emphasize participatory instruction.* The definitions of the concept "mentoring" (Makara, 2002) reveal similarities with the aims and objectives of African traditional education in many respects. The definition contends that mentoring involves a personal relationship in which a relative novice is supported by a more experienced peer in coming to terms with a new role. Both mentoring and African traditional education emphasize "practical training" in the form of active guidance by someone with expertise, wisdom, and authority. The advantage of educating the young under the experienced adult in African indigenous knowledge is that it includes the transfer of tribal mythology, accumulated knowledge, and skills as well as appropriate attitudes. The current shift of adult education from conventional teaching to distance education learning that uses the internet is definitely marginalizing the role of mentoring.

- *Include student learning styles in the teaching.* In the layperson's language, learning styles are unique ways students prefer to learn. Dunn (1990) defined learning styles as ways which an individual absorbs and retains information or skill. This necessitates the inclusion of indigenous knowledge and diversity in learning style in the instruction process. This is important because in essence, the individual has a natural inclination toward certain content and has a natural way of learning. In fact, Gardner (1999) in his Multiple Intelligence discussion stated that human beings respond or fail to respond to learning situations in the world because learning styles characterize these contents. It would therefore benefit adult educators to consider learning styles in their instruction because adults from different areas of the world have different patterns of preferred learning strategies. This will contribute to the promotion of cultural tolerance. Even universal adult education teaching could be more effective if natural ways of learning and indigenous knowledge are considered.

One challenge for the reconstruction of African indigenous knowledge is different leadership motivation factors. For instance, modern leaders are motivated by modernization, hence, the need to collaborate with other countries in order to benefit from the resources and support associated with the implementation of adult education activities. Traditional African leaders on the other hand could be motivated by the need to preserve culture and identity.

- *Acknowledge the diversity of African indigenous knowledge.* Although globalization offers challenges for adult education, it is equally true that it also offers opportunities for diversity if each society/culture is to contribute to the international education system. If adult education is to contribute useful knowledge, it has to act as a vehicle to cultural and social change by validating and enhancing other disadvantaged groups' epistemological experiences. For example, universality would have to be adapted where necessary to strengthen indigenous knowledge systems. As mentioned, there are common understandings across the knowledge systems. Since the world is becoming a global village, it is therefore crucial that citizens of the world learn about each other so that they can coexist in peace and harmony.

SUMMARY

This chapter has argued that although adult education has a social function in the mission and tradition of the discipline, it has overvalued objective truth associated with Western countries' epistemologies while undervaluing knowledge arrived at through connection and personal experience associated with African indigenous knowledge systems. The chapter has also used Botswana as a case to demonstrate the contribution that can be derived from the African indigenous knowledge systems if adult education is to truly support the construction and acquisition of useful knowledge. African indigenous knowledge is perceived as more vital than ever before in identifying and opening spaces where challenging and imaginative thinking can be formed, because it emphasizes the role of collective participation and critique in the production of knowledge.

The chapter argued that African indigenous knowledge should be reconstructed based on empirical evidence of essential issues such as its relationship with information and communication technology. Finally, the chapter recommended that the diversity of these African knowledge systems should be acknowledged and universality be adopted where necessary to strengthen African indigenous knowledge.

REFERENCES

Adeyinka, A. A. (1991). The impact of foreign culture on African education. *Nigeria Journal of Educational Foundations, 2*(2) 7–18.

Briton, H. (1996). *The modern practice of adult education: A postmodern critique.* Albany: State University of New York Press.

Brown, J. T. (1921). *Circumcision rites of the Bechuana tribes.* Botswana National Archives, S. 190/6/1

Brown, M. M. (2001). Can ICT's address the needs of the poor? Commentary, *Voices, 4,* 21–23.

Chilisa, B. (2001). Research within post-colonialism: Towards a framework for inclusive research practices. Unpublished research paper. Department of Educational Foundations: The University of Botswana (1–24).

Cunningham, B. (1997). Ubuntu urged for South Africa's constitution: First black woman in constitutional court advocates traditional social philosophy. *University of Buffalo Reporter, 29,* 6–12.

Datta, A. (1984). *Education and society: Sociology of African education.* London: Macmillan.

Dunn, R. (1990). Cross-cultural differences in learning styles of elementary students from four ethnic backgrounds. *Journal of Multicultural Counseling and Development, 18*(2), 68–93.

Fafunwa, A. B. (1971). *New perspectives of African education.* London: Macmillan.

Gardner, H. (1999). *Intelligence reframed: Multiple intelligences for the 21st century.* New York: Basic Books.

Gathu, K. (2003). Globalization, ICT and knowledge systems: Can developing countries in Africa benefit? In E. Mazibuku. W. Sukati, and K. Gathu (Eds.), *Proceedings of the 10th BOLESWA Educational Research Symposium,* held at the University of Swaziland, Manzini, July 31-August 2, 2003. 197–212.

Grenier, L. (1998). *Working with indigenous knowledge: A guide for researchers.* Ottawa: International Development Research Center.

Gumede, S. (1996). Ubuntu-unanity.http//melt2000.com/releases .bw084/bw084.html

Lange, A. M. (1997). Ubuntu LO13461.http://www.learning-org .com.97.05.0042.html

Lincoln, B. (1981). *Emerging from the Chrysalis: Studies on ritual of women's initiation.* Cambridge, Massachusetts: Harvard University Press.

Magagula, C. M., & Mazibuka, E. Z. (2004). Indigenization of African formal education system: The African symposium: An on-line educational research journal. A publication of the *African Educational Research Network*, 4(2) pp.1–9.

Makara, K. (2002). Management of indigenous knowledge in Lesotho: Prospects and challenges for information professionals. Paper presented at SCECSAL in Gauteng, July 15–18, 2002.

Mautle, G. (2001). Formal education among peoples of Botswana before 1840. *Mosenodi*, 9, (2), pp. 25–33.

Monyatsi, P. P. (2004). A proposal to establish a teacher pilot mentoring scheme (TPMS) for pre-service teachers in Botswana: The case of the University of Botswana. In E. Mazibuku. W. Sukati, and K. Gathu (Eds.), *Proceedings of the 10th BOLESWA Educational Research Symposium*, held at the University of Swaziland, Manzini, July 31-August 2, 2003.

Morolong, B. L. (1996). *Indigenous knowledge and development: Any space for this in the provision of adult education and social transformation.* Paper presented at an International Conference on Adult Education and Social Transformation held in Maseru, Lesotho, 10–13 April, 1996.

Ocitti, J. P. (1988). Indigenous education today: The necessity of the useless! *Proceedings of a workshop on indigenous knowledge and skills held in Thailand.* Bankok: CUSRI and CESO.

Preece, J., & Ntseane, P. G. (2003). HIV/AIDS awareness intervention strategies for sustainable health in Botswana. In B. Chilisa, L. Mafela, and J. Preece (Eds.), *Educational research for sustainable development.* Gaborone: African Books Collective. (pp. 148–166).

Quigley, A. (2000). Adult education and democracy: Reclaiming our voice through social policy, In Arthur Wilson and E. R. Hayes (Eds.), *Handbook of Adult Education and Continuing Education* (New Edition). San Francisco: Jossey Bass (pp. 208–223).

Segall, A. (2002). *Disturbing practice: Reading teacher education as text.* New York: Peter Lang Publishing.

Welton, M. R. (1995). *In defence of the life world: Critical perspectives on adult learning.* Albany: State University of New York Press.

CHAPTER 8

Liberation Theology and Learning in Latin America

Simone C. O. Conceição and
Augusto Marcos Fagundes Oliveira

Somewhere in an urban area of Brazil a group of church base community leaders meet with local people in a church room to facilitate a discussion on the current unemployment issues affecting the community. Members of the local community bring newspaper articles with the latest information about unemployment to be used in the discussion as a resource to share knowledge and start the discussion. The meeting starts with introductory group activities. Then each person who brought newspaper articles presents the information. Facilitators encourage community members to look at the root causes of unemployment, reflect upon it, and then react to the issues affecting the lack of employment locally. Everyone participates in the discussion sharing their own personal history related to unemployment, how it has affected the community as a whole, and what strategies individuals can use to overcome unemployment issues.

In Latin America, learning and knowledge are embedded in everyday practices, as the example above portrays. Learning takes place in different forms and shapes, and for the most part it is invisible because it is undocumented or because it is not clearly recognized as learning or knowledge. Learning is not confined to a particular period in life; it is lifelong (Torres, 2004). In addition, learning is not restricted to formal education, which is classroom-based and connected to recognized educational institutions; rather it focuses on non-formal and in-formal education offered by organized educational activities outside the established formal system, such as in after-school programs, community-based organizations, church sites, or at home. Further notions of learning and knowledge are shaped by the liberation theology context. Therefore, this chapter de-scribes how learning and knowledge are shaped by liberation theology and discusses implications for the practice of adult education in Latin America.

LIBERATION THEOLOGY: A CALL FOR ACTION AND CITIZENSHIP

Political and socioeconomic factors have increased poverty and reduced literacy in Latin America. For example, Brazil en-dured a military dictatorship from 1964 until 1985, which led to economic stagnation. The largest country in South America with vast agricultural and mineral resources and modern indus-trialization, Brazil has endured inflation, unemployment, cor-ruption, and massive foreign debt for decades. Peasants in rural areas and people who live in slums in some of Brazil's largest cities remain poor and, during periods of military rule, their lives became even worse. Human rights were violated; a pattern of disappearances, torture, political assassinations, and attacks on nongovernmental organizations were all carried out by mili-tary dictatorships. Brazilian society suffered as a whole, espe-cially the poor. At this point in time the church opted to take a position to help the poor and oppressed (Le Breton, 1993). In the 1960s, many Roman Catholic priests started approaching the poor. Pastoral workers were thus challenged by new ques-tions and issues. Liberation theology was an outgrowth of these workers' efforts to understand the reality of the poor (Berry-man, 1987b).

Musto (1991) states that liberation theology is "not a new theology, but a new *way* of doing theology." He further explains that "its principal agents are not professors in comfortable seminaries in North America or Europe, but the poor and oppressed all around the world" (p. xxv, italics from original). In other words, he tries to explain that the foundation of this theology is rooted in responses to real contexts of oppression, marginalization, and awakening consciousness for liberation. Liberation theology claims to "lead the people themselves to become the subjects of their own history and to apply the principles of Christian tradition of social justice and non-violence to real praxis" (p. xxix).

As part of their mission, church people realized that they needed to be in close contact with the poor and discover ways of sharing in their life. The first step was to live in the same situation as the poor—move to a rural area or barrio, live in a wooden shack, walk hours through the forest or jungle, wait in lines early in the morning to get water, tolerate dust and dirt during the dry season and mud during the rainy season, and so on. Another step included a model of engagement with the poor through grass-roots organizations or community organizing (Berryman, 1987b). These organizations were places for discussion and prayer during a time when people were not allowed to meet together, except in church facilities. Part of the work of church people in grass-roots community organizations included consciousness-raising, facilitating the creation of grass-roots organizations, mediating conflicts between government and the people, and teaching peasants how to read and write (Berryman, 1987a; Le Breton, 1993).

The grass-roots community organizations, widely known as Christian base communities or base communities, involved nonformal and informal types of instruction and shaped learning for the poor in Latin America. Berryman (1987b) says that "the base communities are a primary embodiment of Liberation Theology" (p. 63). He defines the church base communities as "small lay-led communities, motivated by Christian faith, that see themselves as part of the church and that are committed to working together to improve their communities and to establish a more just society" (p. 64). The Christian base communities were initially created as a way to expand the work of a profes-

sional clergy spread too thin; there were too few priests for too
many Catholics. Also, the base communities were the result of
a set of problems the Catholic Church experienced.

In Brazil, where 80% of the population claims to be Catholic, 5% or fewer of the people attend Sunday mass. Catholicism had little to do with the rites and doctrines of the church;
rather it was more focused on prayers to saints and, in addition,
other religious groups started to expand everywhere. During the
1970s and 1980s, the church base communities were groups of
15 to 40 parishioners that met regularly to discuss the new social teachings of the church. It is estimated that by the late 1980s
there were more than 100,000 such communities (Foley, 1999)
and today there are 1.8 million people in Brazil involved with
the church base communities. Instead of focusing exclusively on
Sunday Masses, the Christian base communities became a place
where faith was made personal.

The base community approach can be defined in the same
way Hammond (1999) describes popular education: "education
of, by, and for the people—organized by people in their own
community, outside of the control of the official education system" (p. 69). In Latin America, this type of education, influenced by liberation theology, offers a number of characteristics:
the focus of learning is on the collective and the individual;
learning is embedded in experience; the community is the source
of knowledge; response to a need is expressed by an organized
group; relationships between facilitators and participants are
horizontal; and group involvement is paramount in the learning
process.

THE IMPACT OF LIBERATION THEOLOGY
ON LEARNING AND KNOWLEDGE

Liberation theology is a theology that is committed to the
poor and oppressed. It is in constant search to provide human
dignity for those whose basic dignity and rights are denied. It
is a theology that is no longer the opium of the people; rather it

is the source of hope and liberation through a dialogical process and lasting self-reflection and consciousness-raising.

The educational process related to liberation theology is based on actions and issues of survival. According to May (1986), the church is changing—sectors of the Catholic and Protestant churches have become more involved in struggles for agrarian reform, justice, and human rights. This process is characterized by Bogo (2003) as a "handful of paradoxes" that brings together poverty and misery, political expressions and actions, and social and spiritual struggles.

The spiritual component of this process is founded on the concept of reviewing and revisiting the individual in his or her fullness as a human being. Spiritual experiences with God or the supernatural change traditional views of teaching and learning as the transmission of knowledge, and conceive knowledge as sharing, experiential, and dialogical. Being part of this process, the individual is capable of infusing values and emphasizing guiding principles of sociocultural action that promote change and encourages martyrdom, self-sacrifice, and the fight for justice. Such actions are the so-called *action for citizenship*, and they amplify the meaning of the social and cultural life of the individual. *Res publica* translated as "the public thing," refers to what individuals in a community hold in common or place above their self-interest. Therefore, learning and knowledge are the result of living in society and fully experiencing the community as a lifelong undertaking, both collectively and individually.

Focus of Learning: Group and Individual

Group learning basically occurs in the organization with poor families, semi-illiterates, or illiterates, who start living with a certain organizational, dynamic, and disciplined model. This model is sociopolitically articulated and strategically thought through as an element of the political struggles, self-affirmation, and self-worth of the group being discriminated or excluded. This practice strongly mobilizes and unites various voices in defense of human rights, equal justice for the poor, blacks, gays and lesbians, Indians, disabled, prostitutes (they are considered professionals in some countries of Latin America), HIV-infected individuals, and other oppressed groups.

As a group the person functions within the process of dialogue and mobilization while individually the person is disciplined and models conduct that is part of a daily practice. There are tense areas in the development of this new way of social living. For example, if groups already possess the cultural practice of living collectively and participating in prayer, meetings, gatherings, visits, and festivities that allow them to publicly dialogue, share, and get involved in collective activities, it is the role of the church person to avoid conflict in these types of authentic sociocultural gatherings. On the contrary, the church person ought to try to carry out the religion by accepting and living with the plurality of forms, reinforcing the group's autonomy and legitimacy, and emphasizing sharing, ecumenism, and sociocultural pluralism. In this case, spirituality is lived by all members of the community through dialogue among different generations—attracting the elderly who can share the meaning of their experiences, and younger individuals who seek to add value to their lives and to the group.

Purpose of Learning

The focus of learning in the base communities is on individual and group experience rather than conveying the doctrine of Catholicism. The purpose of learning is to foster consciousness-raising (or "conscientization"), calls for action, citizenship, and attainment of functional literacy connected to the social and political context of the learner as opposed to objective learning or indoctrination. In analyzing the history of Christian base communities, one may view grass-roots community organizing as originally part of an informal type of learning context where participants gathered to discuss and pray, and then moved to a nonformal type of learning setting through the organization of associations, communities, and unions.

Community as the Source of Knowledge

In the base communities the people are the source of knowledge. Knowledge is learned informally within a one-to-one or small group exchange, through performance, experience, or by example; it is the product of the beliefs passed from generation to generation, community learning, and experiences gained through struggles. Knowledge is learned and perpetuated within the context of the community, for it is shared experience which shapes and gives meaning to the exchange. The main principle is that everyone teaches and learns from and with each other. The motivation to teach and learn is an outgrowth of the commitment to fight together for economic justice and dignity. For the poor, education is a learning, organizational, and political process (Hammond, 1999). To become conscious citizens, individuals acquire the skills to gain critical thinking and confidence in themselves in order to take action.

Response to Needs of the Organized Group

The self-determination of the social groups may sometimes create a dialogue that goes against the church principles. Respect and autonomy are essential in this situation. Liberation theology calls for a response to the needs of the community, and for that it is prepared to create alliances in the present, avoiding contradictions from the past with its forms of domination, which can only create obstacles. These contradictions serve as elements in consciousness-raising and critical reflection to overcome the struggles of the Latin American reality.

Even though liberation theology had enormous influence in shaping the base communities, it is the people's beliefs that affect their thinking, learning, and actions. A good example of a contradiction between liberation theology and the needs of the people in their religiosity involves Christian expressions found in popular religiosity, such as processions, devotions to saints, promises to the Virgin Mary through pilgrimages or penance. While a baptism may mean taking away original sin for a priest, it may represent a medicine against illness or convey a kind of citizenship to the people. In this case, church people and community people may participate in the same religious event with different interpretations. People's interpretation of religious activities is founded on the worldview of their realities and needs (Berryman, 1987b). Another example of people's secular practice having religious overtones involves an Indian chant in Paraguay that affirms God's presence in the middle of the people: *Ñanderú oiko, oiko, ñandé ndivé* (Father Lord lives in the middle of us), a God that shares and walks together with a flock not only announcing the good news, but also making the good news. This does not deal with prayer, but practice.

Relationship between Facilitators and Learners

Important aspects of the base communities concern the participatory nature of gatherings, meetings, and direct instruction, and the horizontal relationship between facilitators and learners. When the base communities began, church people functioned as facilitators, mediators, and educators. As facilitators, during meetings church people encouraged participants to look at the root causes of a problem, reflect upon it, and then react to the problem. In rural areas, a discussion would go from pressing problems related to land tenure to class structure. This discussion would cause consciousness-raising and then lead to the creation of organizations. Church people did not take roles as leaders or spokespersons for the rural people, but stimulated individuals to create and manage their own organizations such as cooperatives, barrio associations, and peasant leagues. These organizations resulted in improvements and put pressure on government officials for needed services (Berryman, 1987a).

As mediators, clergy played political roles in conflict negotiation with government leaders. In 1981 Salvadoran Archbishop Arturo Rivera y Damas delivered proposals from the Farabundo Marti Liberation Front (FMLN) to the government. His role was critical in making negotiations acceptable, despite the opposition of the army and the Reagan administration. Another example of clergy people playing the role of negotiators occurred during 1988–92 in Guatemala. Rodolfo Quezada Toruno of Zacapa (Berryman, 1987a), currently the Cardinal-Priest of S. Saturnino, was a key figure in mediating peace in Guatemala's 36-year civil war. From 1988 to 1992 he headed the National Reconciliation Commission which brought about peace between the military and the guerillas. Mediators work at the macro and micro levels. At the macro level, they work with indigenous people assisting in negotiations against lumber and farmer groups, or helping landless farmers in the process of invading and occupying lands through mobilization and social action. The procedure involves sensitization and search for dialogue with the diverse social sectors, creating the possibility of disseminating permanent action. At the micro level, these mediators act in subtle daily negotiations. The two examples at the beginning of this chapter depict two subtle daily negotiations. Mediators participate in casual meetings such as gatherings where community members drink, eat, sing, and dance together. These elements are part of the ritual that pulls people together.

As educators, the pastoral work of the church was based on a model of engagement with the poor informed by the work of Paulo Freire. Freire's (1970) work provided a methodology that helped the oppressed to identify and deal with the sources of their oppression and become functional literate individuals. Freire's approach to education is aimed at avoiding paternalism and promoting consciousness-raising (Foley, 1999), as well as achieving relevant and useful skills to function in everyday life.

Nowadays, participants or agents of the base communities may be priests, pastors, female leaders, midwives, devotees or faith-healers, artists, or prayer groups that help disseminate knowledge by providing information, diagnosing, and mapping in the same way they collaborate in inviting people to facilitate the meetings. Then who can teach to read and write, who can assist and facilitate? Anyone who has previous knowledge about a topic or theme and knows how to demonstrate it socially. Teaching is not only to show people how to hold a pencil and write on a piece of paper. Teaching does not mean showing people how to draw a letter that will consequently form a word.

The sociocultural agents involved in the teaching-learning process are obligated to respect and understand the different levels
of consciousness among the group members, and in turn know
how to interpret the limitations of the people. These sociocultural agents are part of so-called *catalyst groups*.

Bogo (2003) defines the catalyst group as the group formed
with the purpose of promoting, organizing, and speeding up social chemistry to make something happen. The term "catalyst"
comes from chemistry and is used with the intent to serve as a
substance used to speed up or to delay an event, to modify the
speed, and to intervene socially. Catalyst groups have been in
existence since the military dictatorships during the Cold War
as action groups. They have acted as dialogic bridges between
church communities and society since the 1960s through sensitization and protection of human rights. Later the catalyst
groups used political approaches to pressure the government
through organized civil society. Since the 1980s they have played
diverse roles as political agents and multipliers with the purpose
of articulating and raising social issues, sensitizing, alerting, and
raising awareness of the local reality. Catalyst groups are found
in different environments and may be based on sociocultural,
urban, rural, age-related, racial, ethnic, indigenous, and gender-
based needs of the community. Today the catalyst group is also
used at the university level in action research and as an entre-
preneurial strategy.

Group Involvement Is
Paramount in the Learning Process

How is the call for action and citizenship processed? Group
involvement in planning, preparation, and action is part of the
typical process. The learning process may take an informal or
nonformal aspect. Informal learning may occur through theater,
drama, comedy, and collective songs, where there is an opportunity to reinforce a theme to be discussed. In this context,
participants make commitments, set agendas, pledge actions,
take a position, and share their work socially. At this time the

group memory is revisited by new elements that activate the consciousness and alert individuals to new conflicts and social risks, legitimizing the oral knowledge, and revisiting and recreating ties of friendship and kinship that have been passed from generation to generation—through ties being formed in the present. These ties create opportunities to live together in society.

Each social agent in the process becomes a multiplying agent who recalls group histories, sets meetings together as a group, and pays visits to other citizens. This is all part of life in community, as well as teaching of popular education. Political education is disseminated through collective knowledge found in recipes, embroidery, arts and crafts, dances, and songs. During community meetings in which participants use collective knowledge, topics such as identity affirmation, human rights, social justice, and legitimization of political struggles are incorporated into the learning process.

During this learning process, there is space for solidarity as well as for the development of cultural identity and diffusion of political and organizational principles. Members of this space may be teachers, learners, teaching assistants, and coordinators. The reality is unique for each group. Each group directs its own educational models. Knowledge is learned through practice, experience, instruction, discipline, sensitivity, and attitudes that reinforce solidarity. These attitudes are reinforced to intensify actions that allow the individuals involved, including the destitute ones, the possibility and reality to decode the world around them. The outcome of this process is adult literacy, the creation of mother's clubs and art groups, and the creation of citizenship schools or family schools that work with popular and citizenship practices in different Latin American countries.

The basis for the process that guides the work of the catalyst group is explained by Ho Chi Minh: "People who do not count with their own forces, and only wait for the help of others, do not deserve to be independent" (Bogo, 2003, p. 62). Bogo (2003) describes the catalyst group using a metaphor based on two radios: the wall radio and the portable radio. The wall radio is internal to the community and is composed of leadership within the community, people who live the social problem on a daily basis. The portable radio represents the leadership which moves from community to community. Thus the two types of radios differentiate how people receive messages in the community.

The members of the catalyst group have the responsibility to inform the masses, distribute tasks with a set of criteria, value the militants as well as the masses, be careful of the way they present themselves according to the dress code of the group or the local dress code, and demonstrate satisfaction and enthusiasm to work with the masses. Sometimes these members use lyrics in songs that have content matching the topic of the meeting.

In order to start the process, the agent working with the group must discover the communication point of entry and empathy, as well as compassion with the community, the key approach between liberation theology and the group.

Each group has its own reality. This reality is based on the attitude of the people—how they were raised; how they socialize or live in community; their knowledge of the climate of the region (i.e., types of crops available, flora, geographic agents, rivers, mountains), and knowledge of the calendar of celebrations, cults, family tree, and so forth.

For each meeting, people are asked to bring articles that can be used in the construction of the work and sharing of knowledge. Even in a short meeting, such as a visit, someone will bring a piece of cake or fruit, but this meeting will serve as a stepping stone for future and bigger meetings. If the meeting is part of a leadership training program, people will bring sheets, plates, utensils, cups, mattresses, and hammocks. For each group someone will be responsible for preparing the food.

During the program, the session starts with a formal discussion about the leadership program schedule, schedule modifications, and relationship between learning and knowledge. A typical meeting starts with introductory songs and group activities where group members introduce themselves in a casual way. Then each group shares its weaknesses and histories. At this point the elderly have a special place in the meeting, because together with the meeting facilitators, they instruct the others. A space is then opened for younger individuals who gain respect and status as agents or disseminators once they understand the new norms of conduct and group behaviors.

These norms of conduct and group behaviors are part of the awareness of the internal, external, intragroup, and intergroup worlds and involve legal, moral, aesthetic, organizational, and ecological knowledge learned through practice (everything we do in everyday life). Individuals learn through experience by understanding mistakes and successes; through science by understanding the reality, practice, and veracity of knowledge; through culture by valuing how the roots of the people can replicate the positive aspects and avoid the negative ones; and through discipline by respecting the commitment individuals have to the community in synchrony with the collective construction of knowledge.

For each meeting, there are cultural activities such as "cultural night." In this activity, one may use the meaning of a lit fire, materially or symbolically, or group chat, which announces hope and well-being. It is during this time that people learn how to dance, prepare typical food of the region, share stories, and listen to the diversity of current memories.

Once there is ownership of intra- and inter-group knowledge to exercise citizenship, books, readers, promotional materials, and advertisements are developed. These materials are used to broaden the group and community actions; their main purpose is to promote, disseminate, and preserve the community memory; tell the history to others; acknowledge the social movement; and serve as an alternative fundraising tool for raising funds for the community and movement. Among those involved in developing these materials, it is difficult to know who at each moment contributed to their own silent development: education is like a tree, mirroring the growth and development of people and the community. As the tree needs soil, water, wind, and animals, the people and the community must notice that there are elements surrounding them that follow this analogy. The roots of the Christian base community are the roots of a tree.

This tree, like any tree, is built based on the functionality, freedom, autonomy, and trust that each part should have with each other. This is achieved by directing actions and training programs in concert with the actions of the masses. But caution must be taken. Participants need to avoid dogmatizing organizational forms, methods, and ideological conceptions. They need to understand discipline not as a simple gesture of obedience to the norms but instead as the conscious duty to maintain respect and achieve proposed objectives and they need to know how to respect cultural values of the people and their conduct. Bogo (2003) states that in certain moments during training one may realize that if someone questions or confronts others in the meeting it is not done with bad intentions, but out of curiosity and insecurity. Individuals also learn by evaluation, critique, and self-assessment.

Nonformal learning may occur through advanced adult literacy classes in the base communities. Adult literacy for consciousness-raising based on Freire's (1970) methodology uses materials derived from the real lives of poor people—a small set of words and images from the adult world of the people (for peasants: crops, tools, customs, etc.). These words and images include all the letters of the alphabet and reflect important aspects of the life of the people such as work, poverty, the family, issues of conflict, the possibility of cooperation within a community, and power (such as land tenure). A session may start with a picture showing peasants harvesting a crop. Then, the facilitator may open a discussion by asking what participants see in the picture and encourage them to make observations. Discussion moves to participants' own work, its value, and the problem of making ends meet. Before learning each word in print form, learners reflect on the concept by discussing its significance for their lives. The picture is a codification (observation) of the participants' life experience decoded (reflection) through dialogue. The coding and decoding period may last 45 minutes or longer. After this type of discussion, the session moves to reading skills. The learner is an active participant in the classroom. Through observation and reflection, learners become aware of the causes of their poverty and struggles and recognize that these are not natural realities or the will of God (Berryman, 1987b; Hammond, 1999).

This methodology is so efficient that it is common for peasants to learn how to read in only a few weeks. Learning is contextual, experiential, and meaningful to them. As peasants learn how to read and write, they are able to become actively involved in their own growth, help their community come together, articulate their needs, and organize themselves into associations or unions (Berryman, 1987b). Learning is not just the acquisition of skills, but also the development of the whole person to become an independent and critical thinker.

CONCLUSION:
LIBERATION THEOLOGY TODAY

Liberation theology for education is the art of developing human beings. Individuals leave their condition of poverty to become organized workers and begin the construction of their own destiny, building or giving a new form to themselves by using different ways to shape their consciousness: shifting from physical to mental effort; contributing from one generation to the next; using mass education that involves everyone; using community-based education to sustain organizational work; or using more advanced direct instruction. Implementing this approach to education will hopefully foster better, more participative, harmonious communities and cultivate valuable, independent, intelligent, and open-minded individuals in society.

The rules of living in community open the door to living in a more memorable and broad way because consciousness develops during the whole existence of the human being. The culture is the effort that human beings make to produce their material and spiritual existence to transform the individual and group experience. This experience forms the social memory without local boundaries. There is evidence of results such as these in liberation theology through the creation of social movements in Latin America. Each reality is unique; each group has its own critical and self-critical needs, which support cultural plurality and diverse realities.

Liberation theology has changed since its inception but continues to be relevant as a tool to fight power in society. Bogo

(2003) says that today liberation theology is conducted in two ways: (1) "through the organization, the people, and the utopia of the future" and (2) "through the care for the body, health, and affective relations" (pp. 338–39). In the first case, we can observe the growth of popular movements, the voices of the excluded in Latin America. In the second case it is like seeing education as lifelong learning with the individual learner and facilitator working together to construct healthy social relations.

REFERENCES

Berryman, P. (1987a). Church and revolution. *NACLA Report on the Americas,* March/April 1997. Available at http://www.hartford-hwp .com/archives/40/023.html.

Berryman, P. (1987b). *Liberation theology: Essential facts about the revolutionary movement in Latin America and beyond.* Philadelphia: Temple University.

Bogo, A. (2003). *Arquitetos de sonhos.* São Paulo: Editora Expressão Popular LTDA.

Freire, P. (1970). *Pedagogy of the oppressed.* New York: Continuum Publishing Co.

Foley, G. (1999). *Learning in social action: A contribution to understanding informal education.* London: Zed Books.

Hammond, J. (1999). Popular education as community organizing in El Salvador. *Latin American Perspectives, 107* (26), 69–94.

Le Breton, B. (1993). *Voices from the Amazon.* West Hartford, CT: Kumarian Press.

May, R. H. (1986). *Los pobres de la tierra: Hacia una pastoral de la tierra.* San José: Departamento Ecuménico de Investigaciones (DEI).

Musto, R. G. (1991). *Liberation theologies: A research guide.* New York: Garland.

Torres, R. M. (2004). Lifelong learning in the South: Critical issues and opportunities for adult education. Article No. SIDA4303en. Available at http://www.sida.se/sida/jsp/sida.jsp?d=118&a=3344&language=en US

CHAPTER 9

Adult Learning from a Confucian Way of Thinking

Youngwha Kee

Confucianism is part of our world cultural heritage, the cornerstone of traditional Chinese and Korean culture and an integral part of contemporary Korean life. It is a complete ideological system created by Confucius, also known as Kung-futze who lived in 551–479 BC. He is known as Kongja in Korea. Confucianism is founded on four cardinal principles which guide people to live in morally right ways in the world. They are "humanity, love," "faithfulness and justice," "propriety, rite, or ritual," and "wisdom" (Jones, 2000, p. 2). Confucianism dominated a feudal society that in essence has lasted 2000 years, and for that reason its influence over the history, culture, and the people of East Asia cannot be overlooked.

CONFUCIANISM

Confucianism will be briefly introduced from macro, micro, and international perspectives. If seen from a macro perspective, Confucianism can be considered a religious, philosophical, or cultural orientation. According to Graham (2003), Confucianism is not so much a religion as a philosophy of statesmanship, purporting to maintain the solidarity of the state by dictating the norms for human relationships. Others, however, understand that Confucianism is a living religion and a way of cultural formation: its religious dimension is accompanied by philosophy, ritual theory, historical studies, poetic craft, and painting. All of these form what we call the Confucian way. The Confucian way is a total way of life within the East Asian world (Graham, 2003). Because Confucianism is organized and understood differently from the great religious traditions of the West and Middle East, many East Asians will pause and say that they have no religion because Confucianism has never been defined as religion with initiation or membership. As for a philosophical orientation, the methodology adopted for the analysis of Confucian classics is, for the most part, philosophical. Confucian philosophy is not only historical evidence and an underpinning of culture but also a strong contemporary influence in the modern society of East Asia countries, such as China, Korea, Japan, and Vietnam. As for it being a cultural orientation, in these East Asia countries, Confucians historically created worldviews, ways of life, and deeply shared cultural orientations and sensibilities that are still alive today. Confucians paid attention to art, morality, religion, family life, science, philosophy, government, and the economy. In short, Confucians were profoundly concerned with all aspects of human life, that is culture, and Confucianism gradually formed a complex, holistic, and organized view of human life, nature, character, thought, and conduct (Berthrong & Berthrong, 2000).

Considered from a micro perspective in the context of education, we should know something about Confucius' basic arguments. As a great educator and educational philosopher, Confucius promoted the ideas to educate all despite their social status and to teach according to the learners' characteristics. The first of these broke with tradition as only the aristocracy had the privilege of education. In addition, he took great delight in studying and was modest enough to learn from anyone. He never got tired of teaching his disciples. Besides being a great educator and thinker, he was first of all an intellect with a noble morality. He pursued truth, kindness, and perfection throughout his life and his success and failure were largely due to his character. The essence of all his teachings may be summed up under the first cardinal principle of Confucianism—humanity or love, which is represented by various social virtues such as benevolence, charity, magnanimity, sincerity, respectfulness, altruism, diligence, loving kindness, and goodness. All those virtues help maintain social harmony and peace. Confucius had an everlasting impact on Chinese culture and his ideological system would become the norm for Chinese society. Uniquely, only he is qualified to be called the teacher of ten thousand generations.

There are four basic books of Confucianism on which Confucian notions and perspectives of adult learning are based: *Confucian Analects, Mencius, Great Learning* and *Doctrine of the Mean.* These four books were required reading in order to pass the civil service examinations, which were the gateway to employment in the imperial bureaucracy. Among them, *Confucian Analects* is written by his pupils, and it is the Bible of Confucianism and contains sayings and conversations between the teacher and his disciples. *Mencius* is the philosophy of Mencius and it treats psychology, political theory, and economics. *Great Learning* is a politico-ethical treatise, and *Doctrine of the Mean* is written by Kung Chi, a grandson of Confucius. It is a purely philosophical book. It treats some general principles that concern the nature of the mean and right conduct. These works were put into their present form by Chu His in the late 12th century. Although *Great Learning* mainly focuses on the Confucian way of learning, the other three books also contribute to Confucian thought on learning.

Confucianism can also be considered from an international view. As we know, Confucianism is an international religious and philosophic movement. It spread from China into Korea, Japan, and Vietnam, and has an active part in the lives of these countries' people. Moreover, it is creatively developed in unique ways in each new cultural situation. Among them, the case of Korea is particularly fascinating. Korea's most ancient religions are Shamanism, Buddhism, and Confucianism. All these played an important role in the country's early cultural development and have greatly influenced thought and behavior. Among them, the thought of Confucius embraced no consideration of the supernatural, except for an impersonal divine order referred to as heaven, which left human affairs alone as long as relative order and good government prevailed on earth. In this sense,

Confucianism was a religion without god, like early Buddhism. Korea has been greatly influenced by China, and Confucian thought was introduced from China as part of cultural exchange between the two countries. It came to Korea in the three kingdoms period (37 BC–AD 668) alongside of Buddhist teaching. The Goguryeo Kingdom was inspired and strengthened by Chinese culture and Confucianism, but initially maintained its own customs and traditions. The Baekje Kingdom, on the other hand, adopted Confucianism. This shaped the administrative system and the culture and arts. Silla was the last kingdom to accept the Confucian way of life at the highest levels of administration. Confucianism in Korea meant a system of education, ceremony, and civil administration (Lee, 2001, 2002). Even today, Koreans can hardly be said to have discarded the customs, habits, and thought patterns derived from Confucian teachings. The legacy of Confucianism still remains a fundamental part of Korean society, shaping the moral and legal system, the way of life, and social relations between old and young.

THE CONCEPT OF ADULT LEARNING

The concept of adult learning is to imitate the virtues of a person in Chu His' 12th century interpretation of *Confucian Analects*. According to Chu His, a person who does not know how to act in a situation will follow the example of a person who does know. In the field of Confucianism, imitation of the conduct of the Sages is true learning, instead of gaining some proficient skills (Graham, 2003).

The two Chinese characters *Hak* and *Seb* can be translated into one word "learning" in English. At the beginning of *Confucian Analects*, Confucius asked a rhetorical question, "Don't learning and reviewing/practicing what you have learned everyday bring pleasure and happiness?" (Sung, 1996a, p. 17). Based on this, Kung-futze taught the principle of learning as *Hak-Yi-Shi-Seub*, which represents the enjoyment of learning through daily experience. For him, adult learning cannot be separated from one's daily experience. True learning is being constructed by learners through the inner self interacting with nature. In short, he emphasized meditation to control oneself to imitate those great Sages' conduct and internal integration between self and nature. Especially, *Seub* has the literary meaning of a bird which is learning to fly by the continuous practice of flapping its wings to imitate an example of flapping. *Hak-Yi-Shi-Seub* expresses a constant symbolic relationship with the world around us to feed off of, or learn from, the myriad of situations we encounter as we go through our whole life.

Based on my own understanding, the purpose of adult learning is to be fully human beings. The development or cultivation of fully human beings is not one-dimensional; it must involve experience with and reflection upon many areas of human concern. This relates to another important notion in the Confucian tradition. Confucius characterized himself as a transmitter, not a creator of culture, one who believed in and loved the ancients. There is body of knowledge to inherit to better serve as a cultural transmitter, and Confucius identified it as least five areas which are represented by five outstanding books, that is, *Book of Poetry*, *Book of Rites*, *Spring and Autumn Annals*, *Book of History*, and *Book of Changes* (Skemp, 2002).

The first is poetry, and, by inference, art and music. A human being should not only pursue the immediate and the practical. One should also be involved in the much larger context of culture. This dimension of experience is expressed in the *Book of Poetry*, one of the classics in the Confucian tradition. Poetry, through artistic expression, appeals to the person's internal resonance between the person and the larger world.

Second, most of us, especially parents, know how difficult it is to teach a child to act properly—to walk, to sit, to use the hands, to move limbs in the proper way. This kind of training is called the ritualization of the body. As an art of Confucian education, it finds expression in the *Book of Rites*. Ritual is not an empty, meaningless pattern of gestures forced or imposed upon a young individual to maintain. Nor is it concerned with correct behavior merely for the sake of form. Ritual is a shared, mutually understood system of nonverbal as well as verbal communication. As a socially recognized form, it both preserves and transmits the most authentic human ways of interacting. How does one become acquainted with another person, how does one greet others, how does one smile, how does one show deference? These are simple human acts. It is handed down from generation to generation, and a child must be taught these ritual acts properly to communicate meaningfully to other members of society. Furthermore, there are different forms of ritual and different ways of relating to others. We have to teach the child the ritual corresponding to the proper time and to the proper context. Doing so facilitates nonverbal communication to the benefit of human relationships. This is why ritual is important in the oldest Confucian philosophical tradition.

Third, history is collective memory to know from what place we come. To have a sense of history is to know and to care about the major values and ideas that have shaped the larger community of which we are a part. To have no history is like being without memory. History, whether it is short or long, becomes significant as we become capable of relating to it, as we come to see in it our own past and enter into personal dialogue with those generations who contributed to the culture that shapes us today. Confucius found such a vision represented in *Spring and Autumn Annals*.

Fourth, human beings should also be thought of as participants in society. One is expected to participate in the polity of which one is a part. Thus, Confucian teachings promote a political vision. One is not only an artistic being, a social being, and a historical being; one is also a political being who should be a responsive and responsible participant in the political community. This vision of political participation is articulated in the *Book of History* or *Book of Documents*.

The final area essential to learning to be human is symbolized by one of the most difficult books in the classical tradition, *Book of Changes*. One way of understanding it is to say that in addition to the poetic vision of the *Book of Poetry* , the social vision of the *Book of Rites*, the historical vision of *Spring and Autumn Annals*, and the political vision of *Book of Documents*, there is also a cosmic vision. Using modern terminology, *Book of Changes* represents an ecological concern, both in an environmental and in a spiritual sense. We see, then, that the classical tradition which Confucius, as a culture transmitter, wants to pass on is richly textured indeed. It has its own form, its own content, and, therefore, its own inner logic and spirituality.

THE GOAL OF ADULT LEARNING— BECOMING FULLY HUMAN

A main concern of Confucianism is how we learn to be human. According to the Confucian tradition, human beings are not born fully human. When born, human beings have a body and mind. The situation resembles that of an oak sprout. When an acorn first sprouts, it is not yet an oak tree. The sprout has a body and a direction of growth. The sprout received that body and tendencies for growth from its parents and from earth. If conditions are appropriate, the sprout will become an oak, and similarly a person will become fully human. Confucian thought takes a humanistic orientation and advocates a humanistic way of life. Humans should realize that living simply as a person is not sufficient; one should generate the will to become fully human, which is the task of *Great Learning* of which the opening sentence states: "The way of learning to be great consists of the following: to cultivate the people, to love the people, and to rest in the highest excellence" (Sung, 1996c, p.23).

In *Great Learning*, Confucius revealed a seven-step process, step by step, to attain self-development and reach a state of highest excellence. The order of development which Confucius set forth begins with the investigation of things, the extension of knowledge. Find out why things are the way they are; that is, why the dependent variable is related to other variables. This is the reality of things, the truth (Sung, 1996b). And since everything exists in an interrelated network, discovering this truth empowers a person to transform his or her attitude, sincerity of the will, rectification of the mind, cultivation of the personal life, regulation of the family, national order, and world peace (Wilson, 2003). Following the above seven steps will allow the application, or bringing, of humanity into normal, day-to-day living and thus one becomes fully human, which is the ultimate purpose of adult learning. In other words, adult learning is a guide to becoming fully human.

It is important to note that adult learning related to Confucianism cannot be used as a tool for achieving some goals in a certain situation. The contents of learning are not related to vocational or skill requirements. Learning is totally focused on spiritual things. Cultivating ethics becomes the center of learning, and the aim of learning is not to develop the rhetorical ability of delivering one's own ideas in the Western sense, but to acquire the ability to make intuitive and holistic moral judgments. The goal of learning is to become fully human, a perfect person who does not necessarily have to master eloquence but must have good ethics. It is this kind of learning that Confucius himself promoted (Cho, 1999).

THE PRINCIPLES OF LEARNING

It is no doubt that *Confucian Analects* comes closest to Confucius' educational philosophy. Based on it, Confucius proposed a complete set of principles concerning learning and studying. In the following part I will try to analyze and classify those learning principles via some quotations from *Confucian Analects* (Ames & Rosemont, 1998; Sung, 1996a).

Peer Learning and No Regular Teacher

Quotation 1:

The Master said that, "In strolling in the company of just two other persons, I am bound to find a teacher. Identifying their strengths, I follow them, and identifying their weakness, I reform myself" (*Confucian Analects*, 7:21).

Quotation 2:

The Master said that, "When you meet persons of exceptional character think to stand shoulder to shoulder with them; meeting persons of little character, look inward and examine yourself" (*Confucian Analects*, 4:17).

Quotation 3:

The Master said, " . . . He was quick eager to learn: he was not ashamed to seek the advice of those who were beneath him in station . . . " (*Confucian Analects*, 5:14)

The above three quotations suggest that we can learn from everyone. Apart from asking for suggestions and learning from teachers or parents, we should also seek advice from those who were equal or inferior to us in position (peer learning), and take pride in doing so. Since no one is born a fully human being, each person has strong points together with weak points. To be a fully human being is a heavy task, although it is not impossible to attain the goal. On the way to it, we should learn from others to gradually develop ourselves spiritually.

Self-directed Learning and Constructive Thinking

Quotation 1:

The Master said, "I never enlighten anyone who has not been driven to distraction by trying to understand a difficulty or who has not got into a frenzy trying to put his ideas into words. When I have pointed out one corner of a square to anyone and he does not come back with the other three, I will not point it out to him a second time" (*Confucian Analects*, 7:8).

Quotation 2:

The Master said to Tzu-kung [one of his students], "Who is the better man, you or Hui [a student]?" In answering his own question, the master replied "How dare I compare myself with Hui? When he is told one thing he understands ten. When I am told one thing I understand only two" (*Confucian Analects*, 5:9).

Quotation 3:

The Master said, "A man is worthy of being a teacher who gets to know what is new by keeping fresh in his mind what he is already familiar with" (*Confucian Analects*, 2:11).

As an educator, Confucius put forward heuristic teaching, and strongly opposed the method of pouring knowledge into learners directly, treating them as passive receivers. According to Confucius, learners should become active participants in the learning process. First, in class, both learning and thinking processes work together, so the learners should be encouraged to think over and consider things or matters around them independently. And then, at the appropriate time, the teacher will serve as a guide to illuminate and enlighten the learners. This can be summarized as self-directed learning. The above quotations also embody the essence of constructivism, that is, new knowledge is constructed and gained by the learners themselves on the base of their former knowledge and experience and the process is facilitated and guided by the teachers. The review and combination with one's earlier experience are a necessary and sufficient condition for moving on to the next stage to gain something new. During the learning process, the learners should be trained to have the ability to know ten from one, that is, find the interrelationship among numerous things. This kind of ability is highly valued by Confucius.

Reflective Thinking

Quotation 1:

Tseng Tzu said, "Everyday I examine myself on three counts. In what I have undertaken on another's behalf, have I failed to do my best? In my dealing with my friends, have I failed to be trustworthy in what I say? Have I passed on to others anything that I have not tried out myself?" (*Confucian Analects*, 1:4)

Quotation 2:

The Master said, "Studying without thinking leads to confusion; thinking without studying leads to laziness" (*Confucian Analects*, 2:15).

Quotation 3:

The Master said, "I once spent all day thinking without taking food and all night thinking without going to bed, but I found that I gained nothing from that. It would have been better for me to have spent the time in learning" (*Confucian Analects*, 15:31).

As for Confucius, he strongly emphasized the importance of learning, and meanwhile, he argued that learning and thinking should go hand in hand all the time and should never break away from each other. The above quotations contain the fundamental assumption of Confucianism, that is to put great emphasis on the cultivation of individual's virtues and ethics, which is one striking feature of its philosophy. Self-reflection or reflective thinking is the basic way for self-cultivation of virtues, and it calls for individuals to reflect on their own words and deeds frequently, to criticize and correct their inappropriate behaviors, and ultimately to achieve the ideal personality or character. Put into contemporary terms, when the learners receive education, in addition to memorizing knowledge, the more important task is to think deeply about what they have learned, reflect on it, and to some extent form their own interpretations and thoughts on it. Those learners who just study and never think deeply to put forward questions will get lazy and are sure to be a failure. This also embodies the essence of today's quality education.

Putting Theory into Practice

Quotation 1:

The Master said, "If a man who knows the three hundred Odes by heart fails when given administrative responsibilities and provides incapable of exercising his own initiative when sent to foreign states, then what use are the Odes to him, however many he may have learned?" (*Confucian Analects*, 13:5)

Quotation 2:

Tzu-hsia said, "When a man in office finds that he can more than cope with his duties, then he studies; when a student finds that he can more than cope with his studies, then he takes offices" (*Confucian Analects*, 19:13).

Quotation 3:

The Master said, "Do not worry because you have no official position. Worry about your qualifications. Do not worry because no one appreciates your abilities. Seek to be worthy of appreciation" (*Confucian Analects*, 4:14).

In Confucius' eyes, an intellectual should not be limited to study alone. He did not want his students to become bookworms, who studied a lot but could never handle affairs appropriately and independently. He encouraged his students to apply what they have learned into social practice, and to get an official position is one way among them. The first task, however, is to learn the knowledge and skills necessary for the position. To put it simply, a key objective of an intellectual should be to make full use of one's ability, personality, and intelligence to do good for the state, society, and the world at large.

THE ADULT LEARNING PROCESS

The adult learning process based on Confucianism is a highly complex process which involves commitment, continuous effort, and a holistic approach according to the *Great Learning*. As we have mentioned above, the purpose of adult learning in Confucianism is to be fully human, which will be achieved through seven steps. The seven steps from the *Great Learning* are as follows:

(a) When things are investigated, knowledge is extended, (b) when knowledge is extended, the will becomes sincere, (c) when the will is sincere, the mind is rectified, (d) when the mind is rectified, the personal life is cultivated, (e) when the personal life is cultivated, the family will be regulated, (f) when the family is regulated, the state will be in order, and (g) when the state is in order, there will be peace throughout the world. (Skemp, 2002)

This learning process is continuous and constructed by learners through the inner self interacting with nature. It is a project that cannot be completed in a limited time frame. In fact, many Confucians contend that the process of learning to be fully human is unceasing. It emphasizes meditation to control oneself and integration between self and nature. The outer side of Confucianism was conformity and acceptance of social roles, while the inner side was cultivation of conscience and character.

For better understanding of the adult learning process, we quote Confucius' several periods of life based on his own situation, which can be considered as a continuing learning process:

At age fifteen I was determined to become a man of letters. At thirty I understood that although one was established, one could still experience times of uncertainty and insecurity. At the age of forty I had no more doubts, thus my inner self had become strong in character and could not be swayed by human attachments. At fifty, I knew the decrees of Heaven. At sixty, my ear was an obedient organ for the reception of truth. At seventy, I could follow what my heart desired, without transgressing what was right. (Sung, 1996a, pp. 34–35).

In my belief, he thus had reached the early stages of self-perfection at the age of forty. After another decade Confucius was enlightened to the meaning of life, that is, he understood the reason for being human and knowing his predestined fate. He understood that he was born to suffer tribulations, to endure the unendurable, and to overcome life's tribulations. He recognized the way back to his origin.

In addition to this, relationship is also a crucial term in Confucianism, which argues that the learning process should be extended through continuous dialogues with others within structures of human relationships. Confucian moral thought is grounded in the concepts of five basic human relationships: ruler and subject, father and son, husband and wife, older brother and

younger brother, and between friends. For example, to be fully
human, we should overcome self-centeredness, which requires
that we continuously interact with the members of our family.

The learning process is a holistic one through self-rectifi-
cation and spiritual study. Learning to be fully human is not
simply learning the skills of a particular profession or becoming
professional in one specific task. We know well that becoming
a musician or an artist involves more than the acquisition of
good technique. The cultivation of musical talent or artistic
sense entails the refinement of personality as well.

THE RESULT OF LEARNING

Perhaps because Confucius lived in the middle of an age
of numerous wars, he focused his vision on a harmonious society. He values learning and considers high achievement in
learning as an honor to one's family and one's country. With
Confucianism, it is natural and honorable to work hard in
learning.

And as we know, among Confucius' own pupils were individuals from virtually all social and class backgrounds, because he maintained that everyone should have equal opportunity in education, and he emphasized that wealth and honor
were just fleeting clouds. It is important to note that "everyone"
in Confucius' time meant males only. As discussed in the last
section of this chapter, this priviledging of males is still in force
today in Korea.

In Chinese culture, an intellectual is not limited to study
alone. Confucius roamed around with his disciples; he held conversations with them. An intellectual must know the importance
of ethics when one was to be a politician. In his eyes, the goal
of his teaching is designed to cultivate a man of superior intellectual and moral qualities, and education should identify those
of talent and help them become men fit to rule over others. Confucianism postulates that an individual's cultivation of a good
ethos, a lifetime process of education, is the foundation of the

nation. In brief, the result of learning or education for Confucius served a very pragmatic purpose—to cultivate and create fully human beings who would be able to ensure better government and ultimately achieve the harmonious social order (Reagan, 2005).

RELATIONSHIP BETWEEN TEACHER AND LEARNERS

As we mentioned above, one theme central to Confucianism is that of relationships. He put forward five basic human relationships: ruler and subject, father and son, husband and wife, older brother and younger brother, and between friends (Sung, 1996d). According to Confucius, there was a way or road of righteousness only when fathers were fathers, when sons were sons, when rulers were rulers and when ministers were ministers (Sung, 1996d). Differing duties arose from the different status one held in relation to others. Individuals are held to simultaneously stand in different degrees of relationship with different people, namely, as a junior in relation to their parents and elders, and as a senior in relation to their children, younger siblings, students, and others. While juniors are considered in Confucianism to owe strong duties of reverence and service to their seniors, seniors also have duties of benevolence and concern toward juniors. This theme consistently manifests itself in many aspects of East Asian culture, such as China and Korea, even to this day, with extensive filial duties on the part of children toward parents and elders, and great concern of parents toward their children.

As for the relationship between teachers and learners, the Confucian ideal is quite different from that of Western society. The relationship is based on the Confucian idea that teacher, parent, and king are treated equally and have the same importance in one's life. We know that Confucius and Confucianism attached great importance to the harmonious relationship between teachers and learners, and emphasized the dignity of teachers. Influenced by this philosophy, teachers are respected by the society and learners are asked to obey their teachers. The idea is still prevalent in Confucian educational systems in Korea and China.

THE ROLE OF SOCIETY, COMMUNITY, AND FAMILY IN LEARNING

Mencius, an early Confucian scholar, was concerned with people's individual development, which he maintained took place within the context of human relationships. Ritual and filial piety are the ways in which one should act toward others from an underlying attitude of humaneness. The cultivation of good virtues or humanity is not achieved in a short period of time, and actually it will be influenced by numerous factors. One among them is environment, in both an implicit and explicit sense. Mencius also mentioned one rule for the selection of one's living environment. He said, "it is virtuous manners which constitute the excellence of a neighborhood. If a man in selecting a living environment does not fix on one where such prevail, how can he be wise?" (Sung, 1996a, p. 131). Confucianism persistently argues for the importance of a cautious selection of one's living environment and of persons one selects to make friends. There is an old saying that one takes on the color of one's company, so if you live with persons possessing good virtues, you will be positively influenced from what you constantly hear and see. There is another proverb that if you live with a lame person you will learn to limp, so under such circumstances, it gets harder to develop one's own humanity and good character. Mencius himself provided us a vivid example for the truth. Mencius' mother moved their home three times, and the only purpose was to find a good living environment for Mencius' self-development and cultivation of virtues. So based on the above discussion, it is easy for us to infer the important role the society, the community, and the family have played in an individual's development process.

CONFUCIANISM TODAY

Confucianism is so ingrained in Korean society that it continues today to underpin the value system of the Korean people. Many scholars even argue that all systems in Korea society, such as politics, economics, education, and history are linked with Confucianism. In a word, Confucianism permeates all levels of Korean life. Related to adult learning, Confucianism has exerted influence in several ways, such as the relationship between teachers and learners, instructional methods, the centrality of education in people's lives, Korean female adult learners' status, the development of some popular adult learning programs, and the establishment of lifelong learning cities.

First, the relationship between teachers and learners resembles that of parents and children, and king and subordinates. For example, even though adult learners may be older and have higher social status than their teachers, they will respect and treat their teachers as important persons in their life and follow what the teachers have asked. The reason for this is that the learners consider the words from their teachers to be wise, and these adult learners prefer the lectures from teachers as a method of learning.

Second, the instructional method is also affected. Influenced by the rigid relationship between teachers and learners, probably there exists a communication gap between them. The class is teacher-centered instead of learner-centered, in which the learners just passively receive what the teacher has told them, rarely raising questions, hindering the development of deep discussion, not to mention whether the adult learners' potential will be stimulated or not.

Third, Confucianism has impacted how Korean adult learners' value learning. Especially in recent years, more and more adults seek a way to reenter higher education or actively participate in adult education programs. Koreans consider learning as the most valuable thing in one's life because education is the way to make people become fully human. Koreans today also realize that learning is a lifelong process and will be continued until their death. In their opinion, if they are well educated, they are sure to have more self-confidence over others; in other words, a good education helps build one's self-esteem.

Fourth, there also exists an influence on Korean female adult learners' status in workplaces. Korea is a modern society and it is an industrial power, as modern as any country in the world. While there is a stereotype that Korea is a male-dominated society in which females are in a relatively low position and inferior situation, the roles of females are changing rapidly. The contemporary issue of gender inequality in Korea can be found in many settings—the family, the workplace, or in higher education (Hong, 2000). For example, even though male and female workers may have the same educational background, it has become quite common for females to need more years to be promoted than male workers. Take another example, even if males and females have similar educational backgrounds and similar capabilities, when applying for one vacancy, it goes without saying that the male applicant will win. This can be explained by at least three doctrines in Confucianism. One Confucian thought argues that traditionally descent was through the male line in a family for ritual purposes. Another Confucian thought is grounded in the concepts of five basic human relationships: ruler and subject, father and son, husband and wife, older brother and younger brother, and between friends. In the second doctrine, obviously the former one enjoys more privilege or superiority compared to the latter. The third doctrine argues that education is only for males. Obviously female adults are negatively influenced. A task for modern Korean society is how to overcome these strongly embedded values that privilege men and marginalize women.

Fifth, some popular adult learning programs are offered influenced by Confucianism. Korea is country which is deeply influenced by Confucianism culturally. Currently, the arts still maintain major traditions: Korean pottery, Korean tea ceremony, Korean gardens, and Korean flower arrangement follow Confucian principles and a Confucian aesthetic. In Korea, some senior centers sponsor some special cultural learning programs, which, to a great extent, satisfy those adult learners' curiosity, and on the other hand, these programs help sustain valuable Confucian cultural heritages.

Lastly, Confucianism is serving as an engine to develop lifelong learning cities. Currently, 33 cities are designated as lifelong learning cities by the Korean government. These learning cities invest in constructing lifelong learning centers, and hire professionals to manage the adult education programs for the citizens in their cities including children. These efforts can be explained by Confucianism which considers education as the central part in people's life. Confucianism suggests that government officers should make great efforts to offer some chances for the citizens to be educated through their whole life. In addition, Confucianism persistently argues for the importance of a positive living environment. One takes on the color of one's company, so if you live with persons possessing good virtues, you will be positively influenced from what you constantly hear and see. It is easy to infer that the citizens living in the lifelong learning cities, compared to other citizens, are more motivated to participate in adult education programs, because they are stimulated positively by the city environment. Finally, the citizens are sure to be influenced to accept the idea that learning continues until their death.

REFERENCES

Ames, R. T, & Rosemont, H., Jr. (1998). *The Analects of Confucius: A philosophical translation*. New York: The Ballantine Publishing Group.

Berthrong, J., & Berthrong, E. (2000). *Confucianism—A short introduction*. Oxford: Oneworld Publications.

Cho, J. H. (1999). *A study of contrastive rhetoric between East Asian and North American cultures as demonstrated through student expository essays from Korea and the United States of America*. Unpublished doctoral dissertation, Bowling Green State University, U.S.A.

Graham, A. C. (2003). *Disputers of the Tao: Philosophical argument in ancient China*. Illinois: Princeton University Press.

Hong, J. (2000). *Educational inequality in a Confucian society Korea*. From http://users.ox.ac.uk/~koreasoc/academic/dissertation/2000HongJiY

Jones, D. (2000). *Teaching and learning through Confucius—Navigating our way through the Analects*. Education about ASIA, *5*(2). From http://www.aasianset.org/EAA/jones.htm

Lee, J. (2001). *Confucian thought affecting leadership and organizational culture of Korean higher education*. From http://radicalpedagogy.icaap.org/content/issue3_3/5-lee.html

Lee, J. (2002). *The role of religion in Korean higher education*. Religion & Education, *29*(1). From http://fp.uni.edu/jrae/spring2002/LeeSpring2002htm.

Reagan, T. (2005). *Non-Western educational traditions: Indigenous approaches to educational thought and practice*. London: Lawrence Erlbaum Associate Publishers.

Skemp, J. R. (2002). *The Great Learning of the Confucian school*. Illinois: Princeton University Press.

Sung, B. (1996a). *Confucian Analects*. Seoul: The Association of Traditional Culture Study.

Sung, B. (1996b). *Doctrine of Mean*. Seoul: The Association of Traditional Culture Study.

Sung, B. (1996c). *The Great Learning*. Seoul: The Association of Traditional Culture Study.

Sung, B. (1996d). *Mencius*. Seoul: The Association of Traditional Culture Study.

Wilson, J. (2003). *Becoming fully human—A commentary on the Great Learning*. From http://nichirenscoffeehouse.net/dharmajim/GreatLearning.html

CHAPTER 10

Broadening Our Understanding of Learning and Knowing

Sharan B. Merriam

Most of us who have visited non-Western countries or who have had students from these countries in our classes can recall incidents of being puzzled by something unfamiliar or even counter to what we expected. A number of years ago I remember asking a new Korean student in one of my adult development classes to comment on the Korean custom of young adults living with their parents until marriage. She had not yet participated in any class discussions and I was hoping that she'd feel comfortable commenting on something familiar to her. I was wrong. She was acutely embarrassed by my singling her out, could not speak, and merely shook her head "yes" when I rephrased the statement to say, "Is it true that. . . . " I didn't know at the time that Koreans consider silence a virtue, that it is bad manners to engage with the teacher because in so doing you are wasting other students' time, that one might "lose face" and so on. Of course international students attending classes in the United States do learn our ways (Wang, 2006), and I have since learned how to involve students without embarrassing them. This is but one example of how being acquainted with other perspectives of learning and knowing can enhance everyone's experience.

This book has brought together eight non-Western perspectives on learning and knowing. What makes them "non-Western" is that they have roots in cultures and religious and philosophical traditions that pre-date Western colonization, modernization, and Western-driven globalization. While there is variation within and across these traditions, there are some shared characteristics that contrast with Western perspectives. Realizing that comparing and contrasting is a particularly Western strategy, I nevertheless have drawn three themes from these eight chapters that capture some of the points of difference between non-Western and Western perspectives. These themes are: (1) Learning is a lifelong journey; (2) What counts as knowledge is broadly defined; and (3) Learning and instruction are holistic and informal.

LEARNING IS A LIFELONG JOURNEY

Lifelong learning is a relatively recent concept in the West, having evolved from the more formal notion of lifelong education. While certainly some policy-makers and some educators see lifelong learning as a seamless endeavor that spans a person's entire life, it is more commonly applied to educational opportunities for adults after formal schooling. A number of countries have government policies on lifelong education or lifelong learning, most of which reference formal, institutionalized educational opportunities for citizens throughout the lifespan, but most particularly in adulthood. In the United States though, there is no public policy on lifelong learning and certainly no unified funding source. The result is that the concept is shaped by whatever entities take it up. Postsecondary education for example, seems to be in the forefront in shaping lifelong learning as access to higher education for adults of any age and stage in life. The Department of Labor on the other hand sees lifelong learning as access to training to develop skills needed in the workforce. In the West, lifelong learning tends to be segmented into different lifespan components and institutions with political and economic overtones (Boshier, 2005).

This more formal, institutionalized understanding of lifelong learning is quite different from what non-Western traditions mean when speaking of learning as lifelong. Kamis and Muhammad's chapter on Islamic perspectives on learning explicitly discusses a Moslem's lifelong obligation to learn—an obligation that begins with the first words whispered into a newborn's ear and culminates with the same prayer whispered to the dying person. In midlife, Muhammad himself was instructed to learn to read. The Hindu, according to chapter author Thaker, is on a continual journey of learning that leads to being liberated from this world's concerns. Buddhism with its goal of enlightenment also speaks of learning throughout life; indeed, learning continues past this life into "innumerous" lives (see Chapter 6). The Māori of New Zealand, like other indigenous peoples, also see learning as lifelong and intergenerational. None of these traditions link lifelong learning with institutionalized settings. The learning is primarily informal and embedded in the context of people's lives.

Learning is a lifelong journey toward culturally defined goals. Again, there are differences across these eight traditions as to what the goal of learning is; however, none of these traditions espouse what we normally hear from a Western perspective, especially when speaking of learning in adulthood. Western models of development and learning promote a movement toward being more independent; to be in control of one's life and learning. To be a productive member of society is in fact what it means to be mature in our society. So, as we learn we acquire knowledge, knowledge which allows us to function independently, to be "up-to-date," and to achieve a sense of self as competent, knowledgeable, and skilled. We promote self-directed learning as a means of achieving these goals, and we issue certificates, diplomas, and degrees to validate these achievements.

In the systems explored in this book, some very different goals are apparent in the journey of lifelong learning. From a Confucian perspective, the lifelong endeavor is to become "fully human." To be fully human, one must study culture in the form of poetry, art and music, social ritual, history, political theory, and ecological concerns. As Kee writes in Chapter 9, "Cultivating ethics becomes the center of learning, and the aim of learning is not to develop the rhetorical ability of delivering one's own ideas in the Western sense, but to acquire the ability to make intuitive and holistic moral judgments. The goal of learning is to become fully human." Confucianism has a strong civic component in its view of learning. "Fully human beings" were needed to ensure better government and to achieve peace throughout the world (the seventh step in the learning process).

This civic mission is echoed in a totally different part of the world—Latin America. As the authors of Chapter 8 note, the purpose of learning in the popular education movements in Latin America is to raise people's consciousness about their material conditions, and to exercise their rights as citizens in the attainment of a better social and political life. Liberation theology, the authors explain, sees education as the art of developing human beings, human beings who can make a better society for everyone. Speaking of this "civic" mission, Reagan (2005) observes that in many non-Western societies, "this focus has clear political overtones, whereas in others a more spiritual concern is at issue" (p. 249). He goes on to explain that there are checks and balances for challenging the social system: "In the Chinese case we learn that in all relationships the rights and privileges of the educated person are seen in reciprocal terms; and in Aztec society, the higher one's rank, the greater the punishment for violating social norms" (p. 249).

The moral and civic goals of lifelong learning are also reflected in the value of *interdependence* rather than independence. Recall Nah's (2000) finding about self-directed learning in Korea where interdependence was seen as a sign of maturity while independence was rejected as dysfunctional and self-centered. Native American, Māori, and African traditions also value interdependence and see learning as a community-building activity. As Ntseane in Chapter 7 explains about the goal of lifelong learning in Botswana, it is a "collective activity that is supposed to help the individual in the collective to reach the highest level of critically important values to the African's way of life such as *botho* or humanism. By being *botho* or behaving with dignity . . . among the collective, the individual then becomes part of an empowered group of people who are honest, accommodating, sharing, responsible citizens." Further, "to learn is to live usefully and happily with one's family, with one's community, one's society and with the spirits of one's ancestors." Commenting on the African context, Fasokun, Katahoire, and Oduaran (2005, p. 10) note that while of course "no one is exclusively independent or interdependent" and some balance "is struck by each society, in most African cultures the individual gains significance from and through relationships with others."

Yet another variation on the civic and interdependence theme is Islam's mandate to share one's knowledge with the community. The learner is "duty bound" to share what has been learned. This duty extends to acquiring knowledge for communal well-being. For example, "if there is no medical doctor to serve a community, then it is obligatory upon the community to send one or more of its members for medical training, and failure to do so will result in each member sharing the community sin" (Chapter 2). This learning for the benefit of the community occurs in other cultures as well. I recall a discussion I had with a Native American academic with whom I sit on a university's board of trustees. She shared with me that her tribal community had raised the money to send her to college and graduate school with the expectation that she would be heavily involved in their community's education.

Lifelong learning from a non-Western perspective is truly lifelong, seamless and without institutional, age, or formal boundaries. The goals of this lifelong journey also vary from the typical Western goals of independence and personal and economic success. Rather, learning is to lead to enlightenment, to becoming "fully human," and to being an ethical, informed, and caring citizen in the community.

WHAT COUNTS AS KNOWLEDGE IS BROADLY DEFINED

What is it that people learn throughout their lives? Most would say we learn knowledge, skills, perhaps attitudes. In any case there is a recognized knowledge base that we acquire as we learn to function in our respective societies. There are many questions we can raise about this knowledge base: What gets included as worthy of being learned, and what is excluded? In

other words, what "counts" as knowledge and *who* determines
what "counts"? How does knowledge accumulate? How do we
know when someone has learned? In an interesting discussion
of the relationship between the indigenous knowledge of the
Baiga tribe in India and formal school curriculum, Sarangapani
(2003) asks the question of "whose knowledge is selected for
inclusion" and how is it to be "represented" (p. 200). The author also points out the political dimensions of this process by
noting that astrology has been accepted as a subject at the university level because it "has the backing of the Hindu right
which is closely associated with the political party currently in
power at the national level" (p. 200). While it's not the intent
of this chapter to get into a critical discussion of knowledge construction, these kinds of questions underlie the assumptions any
tradition, Western or non-Western, makes about what is learned.

In the West, the knowledge recognized as most valid is that
which has been uncovered through rigorous scientific methods,
codified into disciplinary structures, presented in textbooks
and scientific journals, and then studied by learners in formal
educational settings. Using the field of adult education as an example, while we know that most learning in adult life is informal and embedded in our daily lives, most adults when asked
about their learning point to that which occurs in a formal,
teacher-led class dependent on books and curriculum materials.
The knowledge learned in these formal settings is considered
valid and reliable, and our comprehension of the knowledge is
often assessed through some sort of examination, certification,
and/or credit. This is even the case in the preparation of adult
educators—we train people to work with adult learners through
formal courses, use of standard textbooks, and some form of
evaluation to "certify" that the professional has acquired the
knowledge needed to be an adult educator. As Reagan (2005,
p. 248) observes, this "common tendency in our own society to
conflate and confuse 'formal schooling' with 'education'—a
tendency reflected in our concern with formal certification and
degrees rather than with competence per se—has been far less
common in non-Western traditions."

In most non-Western traditions, knowledge is conceived of

more broadly than that which is based on the scientific method and studied in formal classrooms. There are different types of knowledge equally valued, and much of this knowledge is embedded in the context of one's life. One type of knowledge explored in the chapters on Māori, Native American, and Hindu perspectives is that of myths and legends, told and retold usually in the form of stories and passed from generation to generation. These myths link to present-day knowledge as in the Māori myths of creation wherein the integration of land, sea, and sky has led to respect and caring for the environment.

Several traditions make a distinction between sacred or revealed knowledge and personal or acquired knowledge. Hinduism, for example, accepts two kinds of knowledge—knowledge that is from the world, and thus learning is outer directed, as well as knowledge that is spiritual, learned through introspection and meditation. Islam recognizes sacred or revealed knowledge and worldly or acquired knowledge as equally important for one's learning; there is no real dichotomy between the two as both are forms of knowledge that belong to and lead to God. In Africa, certain knowledge is revealed through dreams and visions. Ntseane describes how if an ailing person visits an herbalist and traditional healer in Africa today, that person may have to return the following day so that the healer has time to access his or her dreams to know how to treat the patient.

In all of these systems, sacred or revealed knowledge is on a par with knowledge acquired in everyday activity, what one might call practical knowledge. Most often this knowledge is structured by a community problem or issue needing attention, by accessing resources, including people and/or materials that can assist in the problem-solving, and by "evaluating" the learning according to the effectiveness of its application to the situation. In Latin American cultures, knowledge is often that which is constructed within and by the community. As Conceição and Oliveira write in Chapter 8, people in community are the source of knowledge. "Knowledge is learned informally within a one-to-one or small group exchange, through performance, experience, or by example; it is the product of the beliefs passed from generation to generation, community learning, and experiences gained through struggles. Knowledge is learned and perpetuated within the context of the community, for it is shared experience which shapes and gives meaning to the exchange." This is not to say that formal education has no place in non-Western systems; in the world of today formal education has become a necessity, but there appears to be more recognition of and value placed on learning that is what we would call informal, in these non-Western traditions. In reference to Africa, Fasokun, Katahoire, and Oduaran (2005) sum up how this knowledge is constructed: "As in other parts of the world, informal learning by African adults involves learning through experience under enabling conditions that facilitate the development of knowledge, skills, attitudes, aptitudes, values and interests. This is done to enhance performance, bring about change or solve practical problems" (p. 36).

While I've addressed above the notion of knowledge being sacred as well as secular, there also runs through some of these non-Western traditions the recognition of knowledge as spiritual. Of course how "spiritual" is defined here is key, and I propose broadly defining it as knowledge that connects the person with a God, a higher power, a state of being, nature, the universe, and so on. Buddhism, as explained by Shih in Chapter 6, is a continual journey toward enlightenment, a journey that requires studying what has been written on Buddhist philosophy, constantly reflecting, and practicing what one has learned. The spiritual nature of this learning extends past this life. Hinduism also focuses on spiritual growth. The goal of learning, as Thaker explains in Chapter 4, is to be liberated from the world, to merge into the Eternal Mind or Soul, through mastering sacred writings, living a virtuous life, and performing certain rites. In other traditions, spiritual knowledge is closely connected to ancestors who might need to be honored (Confucianism), who comprise part of one's identity (Māori, Native American), or who still wield influence in the lives of the living (African).

What is important here is not to precisely define "spiritual" or "sacred" or "secular" or "communal" knowledge, but to recognize what is different about the nature of non-Western knowledge. Wildcat (2001) comments on the "schizophrenic" nature of Western metaphysics. Since knowledge which is valued in the West is that derived from abstract systems of logic and science, faith and belief become problematic. Not so for Native Americans, wherein, Wildcat writes, "essentially tribal, religious traditions offer a stark contrast to the metaphysical schizophrenia submerged deep in the Western tradition. . . . Rationalist explanation is unnecessary if one depends on experience. . . . In the continuum of experience, indigenous people depend on experiential verification, not logical proof" (p. 53). Wildcat goes on to say that "It is not the least bit personally or communally troubling to indigenous peoples that all of our human experiences, especially "religious" experiences, are not reducible to objects or logic" (p. 53). In a similar vein Benally (1997) speaks of knowledge from a Navajo tradition: "Western tradition separates secular and sacred knowledge and thus fragments knowledge. Consequently, some learning is forgotten soon after academic program requirements are met because it was never grounded or connected to life processes" (p. 84). In contrast, "for the Navajo, knowledge, learning, and life itself are *sacred, inseparable, and interwoven parts of the whole*. The quality of each determines the quality of the other" (p. 84, italics in original).

LEARNING AND INSTRUCTION ARE HOLISTIC AND INFORMAL

As the above quote illustrates, there is considerable overlap among the three themes of this chapter differentiating Western from non-Western perspectives on learning and knowing. If the goal of one's lifelong learning journey is to be a developed human being in community with other human beings, then all forms of knowledge might be important in achieving that goal. Likewise, how that knowledge is learned or acquired most likely involves more than exercising the brain in a formal classroom. Although it's beginning to change and we are seeing more attention to different modes of learning, for the most part in the West, we privilege mind over body and rarely consider a spiritual dimension to learning. The focus of learning and education is "a change in a mental state, from one of ignorance, to one of knowledge. . . . In Western education, the highest status is reserved for the most abstract and immaterial learning, irrespective of its utility, and the lowest status is accorded to concrete, material learning, much of which we learn in daily embodied action" (Beckett & Morris, 2001, p. 36).

In most non-Western traditions, the mind, body, spirit, and emotions are involved in learning and always have been. There is no separation of the mind from the rest of our being. In the ancient Indian practice of yoga, for example, the mind, body, and spirit act in concert on the path to enlightenment (Chapter 4). In Buddhism, one must maintain a "middle way," or balance between body and mind in order to pursue enlightenment. There is also the sense of maintaining balance among the three stages of the learning process—reading and studying, thinking and reflection, and practicing Buddha's teachings (Chapter 6).

This holistic perspective is truly congruent with many of these traditions' view of the world and all things in it. For example, in the Māori worldview, everything in the world is alive and all living things are related. Native Americans, according to Allen in Chapter 3, see all life as "a circle and everything has its place within it." Ntuli (2002) writes that Africans, contrary to Westerners, see the world as an "interconnected whole"— humans, plants, animals, spiritual beings, and ancestors are interrelated. Further, unlike Western society which is "constructed of individuals," in Africa individuals are socially constructed, a "thoroughly fused collected 'we'" (Fatnowna & Pickett, 2002, p. 257).

Much of what is learned in these cultures is to maintain harmony and balance in the world. A traditional Native American symbol, the medicine wheel, captures this idea of balancing the four components of a whole person (the spiritual, emotional, physical, and mental). "When each aspect is developed equally, an individual is considered well-balanced and in harmony. If an individual concentrates on only one aspect, the other three suffer" (Hart, 1996, p. 66). The treatment of disease (dis-ease) assumes that the person is out of balance; the more in balance we are, the healthier we are. So too, the concepts of balance and harmony found in the medicine wheel "extend to others, the family, the community, the natural and spirit worlds, to all that is living" (p. 67). Allen comments on the struggle of Native Americans to hold to these values in a world based on competition and conflict: "The most salient thing" that Native Americans need to learn is "how to function harmoniously and respectfully with integrity in what you do and the kind of person you are and you value, keeping a balance between traditional and modern ways" (Chapter 3).

Congruent with a holistic perspective of both the world and learning, the *ways* in which people learn are multiple and varied. Learning embedded in the context of everyday life is valued more than what is learned in formal school settings. It is *in* the experience that learning takes place. Active participation in the rites and rituals and daily life of the community is how knowledge is transmitted and shared. Two techniques in particular seem to be used in teaching and learning in the non-Western tradition—role modeling and storytelling.

In Māori, African, and Native American cultures in particular, one learns from observing others who may also instruct. Ntseane reports that traditional knowledge in Botswana was most often learned by observation, imitation, and practice. "Traditional education involved all the human senses while emphasizing a hands-on approach. For instance, children participated in the social process of adult activities by identification and imitation learned through observing adult practices and emulating them" (Chapter 7). Allen writes about Native American pedagogy wherein the young learn indirectly through "overhearing" staged conversations and through observing, then practicing some skill. Hart (1996) confirms that instruction in Native American communities is on an as-needed basis and often involves role modeling. First, a learner must ask for help. Then someone who has "experienced the task at hand and can model and/or discuss what needs to be taught" assumes the role of teacher (p. 64):

Students may watch their teachers complete tasks repeatedly. When the teacher thinks the student can complete the task the student is given the opportunity to try. If the student does not succeed she is given more time to master the task. Learning is considered a personal journey towards wholeness, determined by the individual's own pace of development (Katz & St. Denis, 1991). After attending a certain number of ceremonies I have been asked to take over certain tasks. As I completed these tasks I was watched to see if I have learned how to complete the tasks. At times I made some errors thus demonstrating that I was not ready. It was not seen as a failure, but that I needed more time for self-development. (Hart, 1996, pp. 64–65)

A somewhat more philosophical role-modeling occurs in Hindu, Confucian, Buddhist, and Islamic traditions. Here the learner emulates sages and accomplished practitioners of the tradition. In both Buddhism and Islam, one not only learns the teachings of Buddha and Mohammad, one is enjoined to model one's behavior after them. Muslims believe that "the prophet is the best model for every Muslim. . . . Muslims learn how to carry their life by imitating how the prophet reportedly conducted his life" (Chapter 2).

A second major way in which learning occurs in many non-Western traditions is through story-telling. Knowledge and beliefs have been passed down through the centuries orally in the form of stories, myths, and folklore. Sometimes these stories are conveyed in dance, drama, and music. At least three chapter authors—Thaker, Allen, and Ntseane—share personal experiences with storytelling and how they learned about their cultural heritage through these narratives. To this day in First Nations tribes, "when someone approaches a member of an extended family, traditional healer or an Elder for help or teachings, they may be supported through discussions, including stories (Hart, 1996, p. 63).

The power of stories, "the oldest and most natural form of sense making" (Jonassen & Hernandez-Serrano, 2002, p. 66), is that they enable us to make meaning of our lives as well as preserving the knowledge base of a particular culture, religion, or philosophical system. Storytelling is a much valued means of learning in most non-Western traditions. There's nothing "scientific" about this way of knowing (also called narrative knowing) as Rossiter (2005) notes in summing up the difference between scientific and narrative knowing: "Narrative knowing . . . is concerned more with human meaning than with discrete facts, more with coherence than with logic, more with sequences than with categories, and more with understanding than with predictability and control" (p. 419).

An interesting aspect of the teaching-learning transaction in these non-Western traditions is the role of teacher. Unlike in the West where most teachers are "trained" and certified to be teachers, in non-Western systems, it is the responsibility of all in the community to teach and to learn. In commenting on seven traditions (African indigenous, Aztec, Native American, Confucian, Hindu and Buddhist, Rom, and Islamic) presented in his book, Reagan (2005) observes that

> The concept of some adults being *teachers* and others (presumably) being *non-teachers* is a somewhat alien one to many traditions. Furthermore, it is interesting to note that in none of the cases examined here—even those with the most fully articulated formal educational systems—was there any explicit, formal training for those who would play teaching roles. The idea of teachers engaging in a profession, with specialized knowledge and expertise not held by others, appears to be a Western, and indeed relatively recent, innovation. (p. 249, emphasis in original).

Even in traditions where the role of teacher is revered, one can learn from various others in the community. For example, Kee cites several teachings of Confucius suggesting that one can learn from everyone. Even people of "little character" can cause us to look inward and examine ourselves (Chapter 9). That anyone can be a teacher or a learner is certainly implicit in the Māori framework. As authors Findsen and Tamarua tell us, the Māori word *ako* means "to teach and to learn"—there are no words to separate these two concepts.

In some traditions the community itself is the "teacher."

Latin American education influenced by the social activist agenda of liberation theology sees the community as the source of knowledge and relationships between community participants and facilitators are collaborative and nonhierarchical. Conceição and Oliveira explain that in these communities the relationship between facilitators and learners is "horizontal": "Church people functioned as facilitators, mediators, and educators." Facilitators "encourage participants to look at the root causes of the problem, reflect upon it, and then react to the problem" (Chapter 8).

African indigenous knowledge systems and Native American traditions seem to have the broadest concept of who or what can be a teacher. Ntseane explains that indigenous knowledge is "stored in cultural and religious beliefs, taboos, folklore or myths as much as in the individual's practical experience." Since knowledge is shared across the community even children can be teachers as attested to in the proverb, "'Don't throw away weeds found in a child's wild vegetable harvest.' The idea here is that what you see as weeds could actually be new knowledge" (Chapter 7). In Native American communities, "teachers are servants of the community" who help bring harmony and balance between the natural and spiritual world (Hart, 1996, p. 65). "Anyone and anything has the potential to be a teacher, including children, youth, adults, the elderly, plants, animals, and spirits. . . . Also, just as everything and everyone is a teacher, they are also all students" (p. 65).

A lot has been written about the holistic nature of learning in non-Western traditions. Certainly the eight perspectives presented in this collection reinforce this view of learning and knowing, a view in contrast to a primarily cognitive emphasis in the West. Congruent with a holistic approach to learning are the learning strategies found in these traditions. Learning is informal, practical, and deeply embedded in the context of everyday life. Much is learned through observation of others and then active participation. The recitation of stories, myths, and folklore is also a valid and accepted way to learn. Finally, teachers are those who can assist others in their learning and are themselves learners.

SUMMARY

This chapter began with the premise that our understanding of what it means to learn and to know can be broadened by exposure to non-Western perspectives on the topic. In turn, a broader perspective can enhance our practice as educators in a world that is increasingly diverse as well as interconnected through travel and technology. To that end, I have drawn three themes that non-Western perspectives have in common. First, learning really is a lifelong endeavor unfettered by institutional or other boundaries. Second, what counts as knowledge is broadly defined, and third, learning and instruction can be holistic and informal. Reflecting on these themes it seems that Western educators know them to be "true" at some level of what learning and knowing can be about. However, our Western obsession with the cognitive domain, with "scientific" knowledge, and with formal schooling from preschool to professional preparation rarely leaves little space in our psyche and our practice for accommodating these non-Western views. The traditions themselves are of course being challenged and undermined in some cases by Westernization/modernization. Most of the authors speak to the place of these traditions in today's world; however, a thorough discussion of this topic was beyond the scope of this project. Rather, it is hoped that by making these perspectives accessible to Western educators, that our perspectives will be broadened and our practice enhanced.

REFERENCES

Beckett, D., & Morris, G. (2001). Ontological performance: Bodies, identities and learning. *Studies in the Education of Adults, 33*(1), 35–48.

Benally, H. J. (1997). The pollen path: The Navajo way of knowing. In Foehr, R. P., & Schiller, S. A. (Eds.), *The spiritual side of writing* (pp. 84–94). Portsmouth, NH: Boynton/Cook Publishers, Inc.

Boshier, R. (2005). Lifelong learning. In L. M. English (Ed.), *Interna-*

tional encyclopedia of adult education (pp. 373–378). New York: Palgrave Macmillan.

Fasokun, T., Katahoire, A., & Oduaran, A. (2005). *The psychology of adult learning in Africa.* Hamburg, Germany: UNESCO Institute for Education and Pearson Education South Africa.

Fatnowna, S., & Pickett, H. (2002). The place of indigenous knowledge systems in the post-modern integrative paradigm shift. In C. A. O. Hoppers (Ed.), *Indigenous knowledge and the integration of knowledge systems* (pp. 257–285). Claremont, South Africa: New Africa Books Ltd.

Hart, M. A. (1996). Sharing circles: Utilizing traditional practice methods for teaching, helping, and supporting. In S. O'Meara & D. A. West (Eds.), *From our eyes: Learning from indigenous peoples* (pp. 59–72). Toronto: Garamond Press.

Jonassen, D. H., & Hernandez-Serrano, J. (2002). Case-based reasoning and instructional design: Using stories to support problem solving. *Educational Technology Research and Development, 50*(2), 65–77.

Nah, Y. (2000). Can a self-directed learner be independent, autonomous and interdependent?: Implications for practice. *Adult Learning, 18*, 18–19, 25.

Ntuli, P. P. (2002). Indigenous knowledge systems and the African renaissance. In C. A. O. Hoppers (Ed.), *Indigenous knowledge and the integration of knowledge systems* (pp. 53–66). Claremont, South Africa: New Africa Books.

Reagan, T. (2005). *Non-Western educational traditions: Indigenous approaches to educational thought and practice* (3rd ed.), Mahwah, NJ: Lawrence Erlbaum Associates, Publishers.

Rossiter, M. (2005). Narrative. In English, L. M. (Ed.). *International encyclopedia of adult education* (pp. 418–422). New York: Palgrave Macmillan.

Sarangapani, P. M. (2003). Indigenising curriculum: Questions posed by Baiga *vidya. Comparative Education, 39*(2), 199–209.

Wang, H. (2006). *How cultural values shape Chinese students' learning experience in American universities.* Unpublished doctoral dissertation. The University of Georgia, Athens, GA.

Wildcat, D. R. (2001). The schizophrenic nature of metaphysics. In V. Deloria, Jr. & D. Wildcat, *Power and place: Indian education in America* (pp. 47–55). Golden, Colorado: American Indian Graduate Center and Fulcrum Resources.